Origami
Handbook

Origami Handbook

Paul Jackson

A QUANTUM BOOK

Published by Grange Books
an imprint of Grange Books Ltd.
35, Riverside
Sir Thomas Longley Road
Medway City Estate, Rochester
Kent ME2 4DP
www.grangebooks.co.uk

ISBN 978-1-84804-012-0

QUMCO22-N

This book was produced by
Quantum Books Ltd
6 Blundell Street
London N7 9BH

Printed in Singapore by Star Standard Industries Pte. Ltd

CONTENTS

INTRODUCTION

What is classic origami? There are of course, many different opinions, but most paper-folders would agree that, the very best origami is enjoyable to fold and attractive to look at. The folding sequence should be economical and flow elegantly from one step to the next, so that the design emerges seemingly effortlessly from the paper and concludes boldly, even dramatically, without any messy rounding off or tucking in. The completed design should not be scarred with unwonted creases, be misshapen or have an unnecessarily complex surface.

Perhaps most importantly though, the design should somehow be original. The restrictive 'rules' of origami (the paper may only be folded, never cut or glued) mean that true originality is rare and most designs, though clever, are often little more than variations on well-worn themes. A classic design must, be a one-off.

If you are new to origami, please read the next few pages before starting to fold. They will make the book easy and a pleasure to use. Experienced readers may wish to skip them, but do be careful to fold within your capability: too much ambition can end in frustration, though it is sometimes fun to try something difficult. Please remember that whether you are a master or a novice, your level of ability is unimportant, so long as you enjoy what you can make. In fact, the very greatest designs are the simplest ones, so beginners take note! It isn't what you put in that can make a design a classic, but what you leave out. In origami, less is sometimes more.

I have had the greatest pleasure assembling this collection of personal favourites and hope that they will delight and inspire you.

PAUL JACKSON

PAPER

There are two types of paper for origami: ordinary paper to practise with and special paper to display your favourite designs. A particularly good practice paper is photocopying paper, which can be bought from stationers or from the photocopying print shops found in most shopping centres. Buy the paper in bulk and the cost per sheet becomes minimal. For a small sum, a print shop will trim the oblong sheets to perked squares, saving you much labour and guaranteeing accuracy. Other excellent practice papers include writing paper, typing paper, computer paper, brown wrapping paper and even pages cut from a magazine if no other paper is available. Avoid folding newspaper, paper tissues and duplicating paper.

A favourite design folded for display will have a greater presence if made from an unusual but appropriate paper. Art and craft shops sell a wide variety of interesting papers suitable for folding, including Ingres (Strathmore) paper, pastel paper, watercolour paper and textured or marbled papers. Some large cities have shops which specialize in selling nothing but paper and these are certainly worth a visit. Oriental import shops and craft shops sell packets of traditional square origami paper, white on one side and coloured on the other. Origami paper is convenient to use and pretty to look at, but it can make some designs look gaudy. For displays, use it with care.

Consider too using unlikely papers: try folding wallpaper, old posters, paper-backed metallic foil, decorative gift-wrap paper, handmade paper or even thin card, cellophane and paper bath mats. Anything goes! Start a collection of unusual papers and experiment.

SYMBOLS

Symbols are the core of any book about origami. They need not all be learnt at once, but it is important to know at least the symbols for valley and mountain folds. When you see an unfamiliar symbol, refer back to this page to see what it means.

valley fold (fold to the front)

existing crease

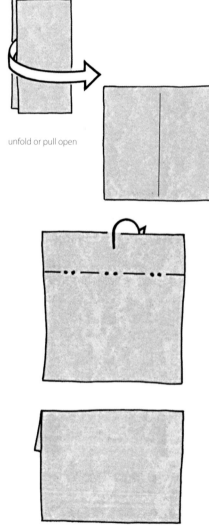

unfold or pull open

mountain fold (fold behind)

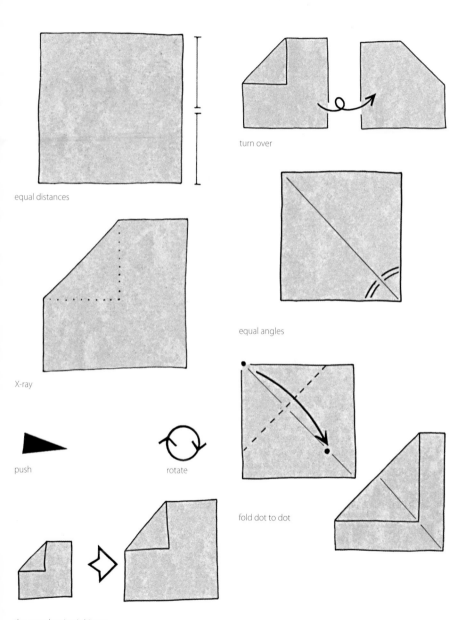

equal distances

turn over

equal angles

X-ray

push

rotate

fold dot to dot

the next drawing is bigger

FIRST PRINCIPLES
How To Make A Square

Most bought papers are oblong and have to be trimmed square. There are several ways to do this, but here is the best.

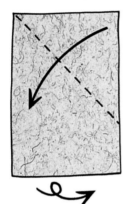

1 Fold a triangle. Turn over.

3 Cut off the excess oblong of paper with a non-serrated kitchen knife which has a blade at least 12 cm (5 in) long.

5 The completed square. Done properly, the edge is pleasingly clean.

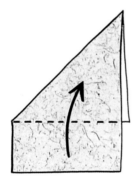

2 Fold up the oblong exactly level with the edge of the triangle behind.

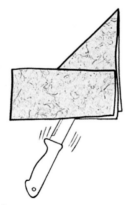

4 Hold the paper firmly against a hard, level surface and cut along the crease with a series of smooth slicing movements.

HOW TO MAKE A CREASE

This may seem pedantic to the eager beginner, but it is important to know how to make an accurate crease. Just one inaccuracy early in a sequence will throw all the later creases out of alignment, creating a clumsy design.

The basic rule is very simple. Keep rotating the paper (or turning it over), so that every crease is made from left to right across your body (or right to left, if preferred), and the part of the paper which folds over when the crease is made moves away from your body, not towards it or to one side.

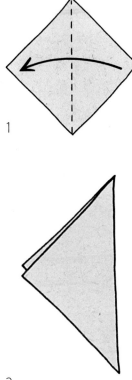

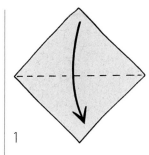

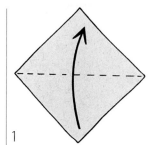

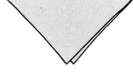

2 A incorrect crease.

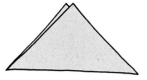

2 A incorrect crease.

2 A correct crease.

When you see a crease on a diagram which does not run from left to right, *rotate the paper* so that it does, then make the crease.

When you see a mountain fold symbol, turn the paper over (or open up the inside), making a *valley* fold, then turn back over (or close up) again.

Creases are not chores to be done as quickly as possible on the way to completing a design. They should be enjoyed. Some experts believe that the pleasure of origami lies more in the making of creases and the manipulation of paper, than in achieving a completed design, or looking at one. Take time out to *enjoy* your folding.

BASIC TECHNIQUES

The root of paper folding is the valley fold (and its opposite the mountain fold). Such basic creases need no explanation, but more complex techniques do. The most common technique is the reverse fold and its opposite the outside reverse fold (most things in origami it seems, have an opposite). They are explained below, as is another technique, the squash fold. Other techniques are explained with the designs.

If you are unfamiliar with the reverse and squash folds, please take a little time to fold the basic examples and studies which follow.

REVERSE FOLD

Basic Example

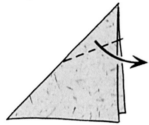

1 Fold in half.

2 Fold the corner across to the right.

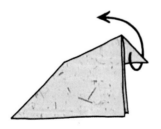

3 then fold it around the back along the same crease.

4 Unfold.

5 Hold as shown. Swing the top corner down between the layers ...

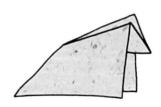

6 ... like this. Flatten the creases. The reverse fold complete.

The reverse fold described on the previous page is notated like this:

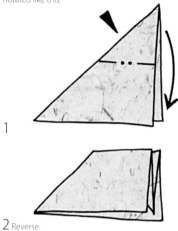

1

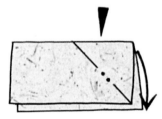

2 Reverse.

STUDIES

Here are further examples. Look at them carefully before attempting them.

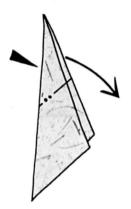

1 Reverse.

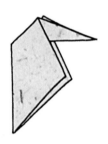

2

If you are unfamiliar with the reverse fold, prepare by folding the crease backwards and forwards as in steps 2-4 of the basic example above.

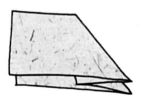

1 Reverse.

2

OUTSIDE REVERSE FOLD

Basic Example

1 Fold the corner across to the left . . .

2 . . . then fold it around the back along the same crease.

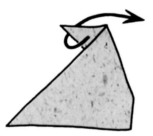

3 Unfold.

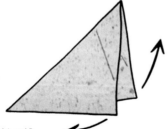

4 Spread A and B.

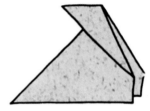

5 Refold both short creases as valleys, lifting C.

6 Collapse back in half.

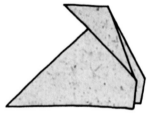

7 The outside reverse fold complete.

The outside reverse fold described above is notated like this:

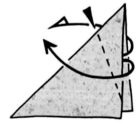

1 Outsider reverse

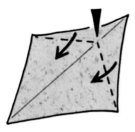

2

SQUASH FOLD

Basic Example

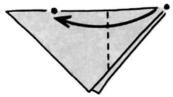

1 Fold in half.

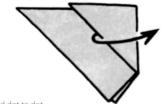

2 Fold dot to dot.

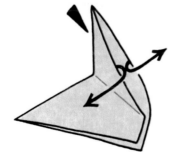

3 Unfold, so that A stands upright.

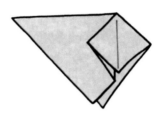

4 Squash A flat, opening the pocket . . .

5 like this. Flatten the paper. The squash fold complete.

The squash fold described above is notated like this:

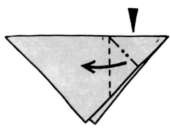

1 Squash.

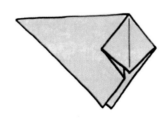

2

TRADITIONAL DESIGNS

Traditional designs are designs of uncertain origin. Nobody knows where they were first folded, when, by whom and sometimes why. Some may be a thousand years old or more.

Curiously, almost all (surviving) traditional designs of note have variations, whereas most modern classic designs do not. The Junk and Sampan for example, can be folded in numerous ways, not just to achieve the same form, but to achieve simpler or more complex variations. Even the elementary Banger and Glider can be folded in several different ways. Perhaps this has helped them to survive: each generation can remember the basis of a design but forgets the detail and so has to re-invent it.

What qualities make the basis of a particular design so memorable? Eastern symbolism aside, perhaps it is because something about that design is unique: the Banger makes a loud noise, the Dish is circular, the Sampan turns completely inside-out and so on. What's more, they all have a clever or entertaining finish to make the folding worthwhile. Origami is very much a performing art.

Some knowledgeable paper-folders have little regard for traditional designs, preferring the fireworks of complex modern creations. However, like popular melodies, these designs have endured because of an appeal more profound than mere fashion. Their simplicity is deceptive, transcending cultures.

BANGER

This is one of the most entertaining of all paper folds and certainly the loudest! Practise Step 7, because good technique will increase the volume of the bang. Use a rectangle of thin or medium weight paper, at least 25 x 37 cm (10 x 15 in). Larger sheets will produce louder noises

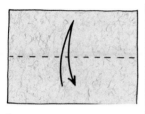

1 Fold one long edge across to the other. Crease and unfold.

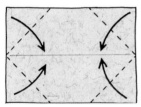

2 Fold in the corners to the centre crease.

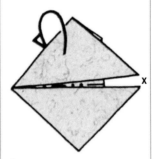

3 Fold in half along the Step 1 crease.

4 Mountain fold across the middle. Crease and unfold.

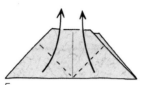

5 Check that the centre crease made in Step 1 is a mountain (if it's a valley, turn the paper over), then fold the sharp corners across to the right.

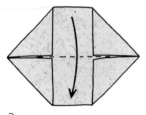

6 Mountain fold in half. Note the double corner at X.

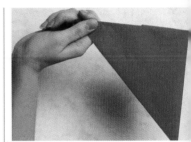

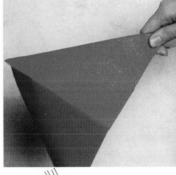

7 Hold X as shown. Bend your elbow so that the Banger is behind your head, then whip it downwards very quickly. The paper will unfold with a loud BANG! If it doesn't, check that you haven't held the paper upside down and try to move your arm quicker.

CROWN

Hats are a popular origami subject. This design creates a large, well-locked hat from a relatively small sheet and because of its square shape it will grip your head well. Use a square of sturdy paper 37 x 37 cm (15 x 15 in) for a child and a little larger for an adult head.

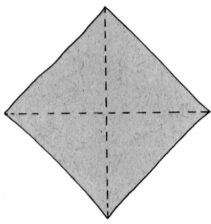

1 Crease and unfold both diagonals.

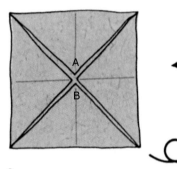

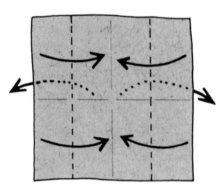

3 Note A and B. Turn over.

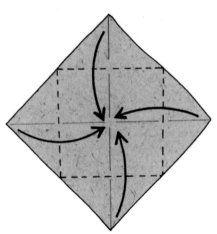

2 Fold the corners to the centre.

4 Fold the top and bottom edges to the centre crease, allowing corners A and B to flip out from behind.

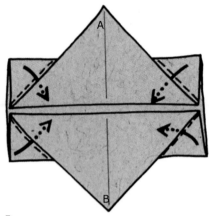

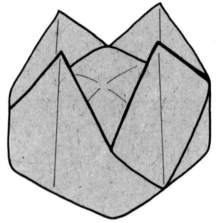

5 like this. Fold the small triangles under the large ones.

7 to complete the Crown. Press it into shape, squaring the sides.

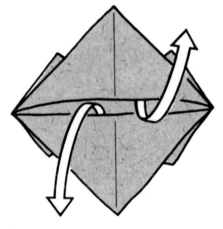

6 Pull open the slit.

BIRD

Whereas some origami designs can be naturalistic, other designs, such as this one, are really symbols. Here is a bird – not a duck or a swan – just a bird: it has a head, wings and and a tail, so it must be one, even though it doesn't look like any particular species. Is the design a remarkable distillation of form, or merely an example of inadequate technique? Surely the former. Use a 15-20 cm (6-8 in) square of paper.

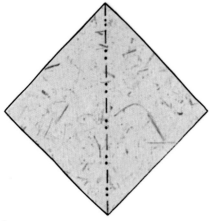

1 Make a mountain crease along a diagonal. Unfold.

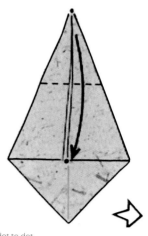

3 Fold dot to dot.

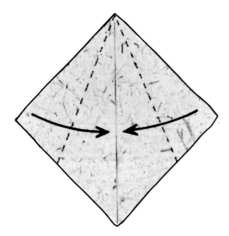

2 Fold two edges to the centre crease. Be careful to make a neat corner at the top.

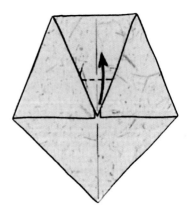

4 Fold the sharp corner back up a little way. The exact distance is unimportant.

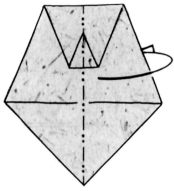

5 Mountain fold in half.

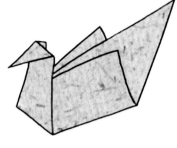

8 The Bird is complete.

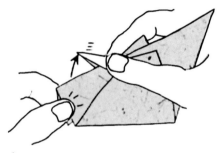

6 Lift the beak away from the neck. Squeeze flat the back of the head to make new creases.

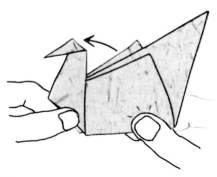

7 Lift the neck away from the body. Squeeze flat the base of the neck to make new creases.

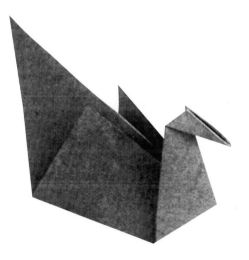

CUP

Few origami designs are practical. Made from a waterproof material such as metallic kitchen foil or greaseproof paper, this simple design will hold a liquid without leaking through an open edge. Turned upside down, it will even make an excellent hat. Flap B can be brought down to form a visor. Use a 15-20 cm (6-8 in) square of paper.

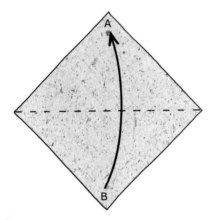

1 Fold in half along a diagonal.

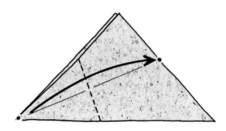

4 Fold one dot to the other.

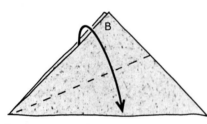

2 Fold down corner B to the bottom edge . . .

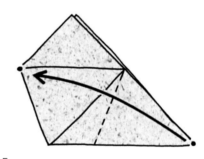

5 Fold one dot to the other.

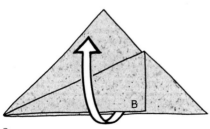

3 . . .like this Unfold.

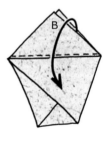

6 Fold down single layer B.

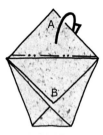

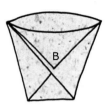

7 Fold down single layer B.

8 The Cup is complete.

WATERLILY

This is the full version of a spectacular napkin fold sometimes seen in restaurants. Note the remarkable manner in which the uninteresting shape made up to Step 6 is gradually opened up and transformed into the beautiful completed design. Use a paper napkin. Ordinary paper will rip at Step 7.

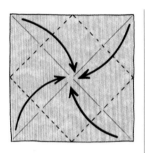

1 Fold the corners to the centre.

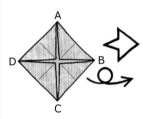

4 Turn over. Note ABCD.

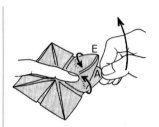

7 Hold as shown. Pull A forcibly upwards, so that it unpeels around E...

2 Again, fold the corners to the centre.

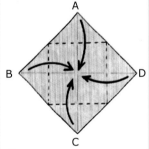

5 Yet again fold the corners to the centre.

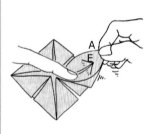

8 ... like this. Repeat with B C and D, keeping hold of the centre.

3 Once again, fold the corners to the centre.

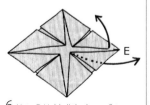

6 Note E. Hold all the layers flat and pull out corner A mentioned in Step 4.

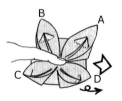

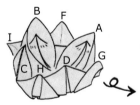

9 Turn over. Note FGHI. Lift F …

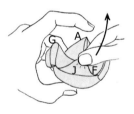

11 Turn over.

13 …and pull it up in front of A. Repeat with K L and M.

10 ..and pull it up between A and B, as far as it will go. Repeat with G H and I, still keeping hold of the centre.

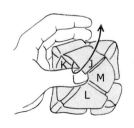

12 Note JKLM. Lift J ….

14 The Waterlily is complete.

DISH

The Dish is unique in origami: it is the only known circular design. What's more, the final shape is very attractive and the opening out moves in Steps 11-12 are particularly satisfying. Use a 15-20 cm (6-8 in) square of paper. For a decorative effect, use a paper differently coloured on its two sides.

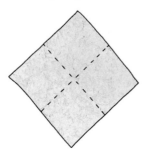

1 Valley fold in half horizontally and vertically, to make four squares. Unfold each crease.

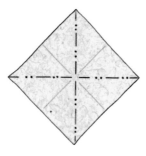

2 Mountain fold each diagonal. Unfold.

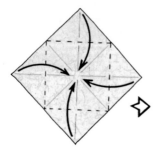

3 Fold the corners to the centre.

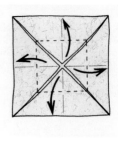

4 Fold the corners back out to the edge.

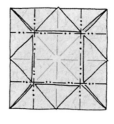

5 Crease and unfold four mountain folds as shown. (It is probably easier to make valley folds by turning the paper over.)

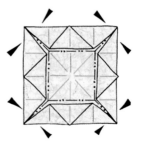

6 Make short mountain diagonals. Pinch the edges near the corners …

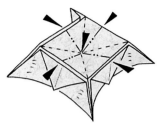

7 ... to raise a table shape in the centre and make the paper 3D. Push down on the centre point whilst pushing the edges of the 'table' towards the centre ...

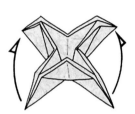

8 ... like this. Note the X shape of the paper. Flatten the X shape with two points to either side.

9 Reverse fold the front corners inside.

10 Repeat behind.

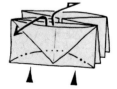

11 Push the bottom edge upwards with a curved crease, so that the top edges of the pocket separate in a curved shape.

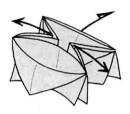

12 This is the result. Repeat on the other three sides.

13 The Dish complete. Neaten the interior edges to make an attractive star shaped central pocket.

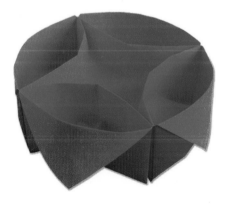

FLAPPING BIRD

Here is perhaps the greatest of all 'action models'. The bird shape is itself satisfying, but the wide, graceful arc made by the wings when flapped is dramatic and appealing. If you want to carry an origami design in your handbag or wallet to entertain people with, this must surely be the one. Use a 15-25 cm (6-10 in) square of paper.

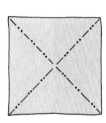

1 Mountain fold both diagonals. Unfold.

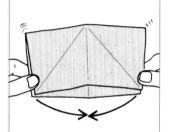

4 Hold as shown. Swing your hands together . . .

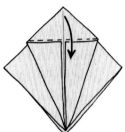

7 . . .like this. Fold down the top triangle.

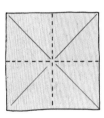

2 Valley fold horizontally and vertically. Unfold.

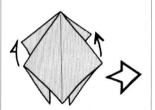

5 .. to create this 3D star shape. If the pattern of mountains and valleys is incorrect it will not form, so check Steps 1-2.

8 Pull out the side triangles.

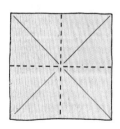

3 Fold the top edge down to the bottom along the existing crease.

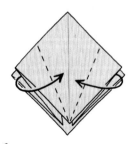

6 With the closed (neat) corner at the top, fold in the lower front edges to the centre crease . . .

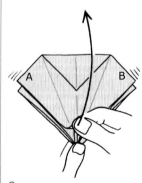

9 Take hold of just the top layer. Lift it upwards . . .

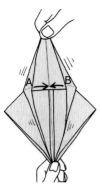

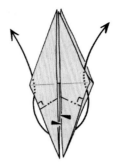

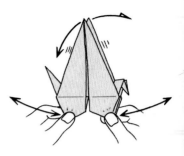

10 ...swivelling it right up and over the top edge of the paper shape. A and B will move inwards.

13 Reverse fold each of the lower points, so that each reverse starts a little below the centre of the diamond.

15 Hold as shown. To complete the Flapping Bird, move your hands gently apart and together, apart and together, and the wings will flap!

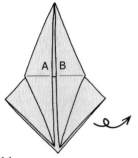

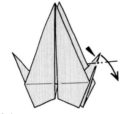

11 Flatten the diamond shape with strong creases. Turn over.

14 Reverse the head.

12 Repeat Steps 6-11 on this side, to make another diamond shape to match the first. Note the loose triangle hidden between them

CRANE

The Crane is the one design that all Japanese people seem to know. In recent times it has become a potent symbol of peace and friendship. Garlands of Cranes strung together in the flat form seen in Step 4 can be seen at many Peace shrines around the world. Use thin or medium weight paper at least 15 cm (6 in) square. Begin by folding the Flapping Bird up to Step 13.

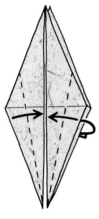

1 Fold the lower front edges to the centre. Repeat behind. Be careful to make the bottom corners neat and sharp.

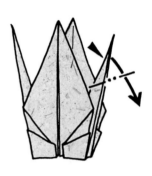

3 Reverse the head.

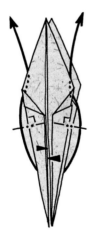

4 Pull the wings apart, squashing the central hump.

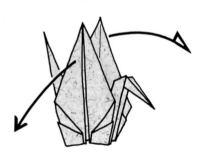

2 Reverse fold the lower spikes.

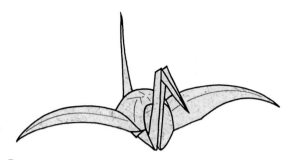

5 The Crane is complete.

GLIDER

What could be simpler – a Glider with only two folds! Be careful to follow the instructions carefully, because it is important to hold and release it in the correct way. There is probably an even simpler Glider with just one crease, waiting to be designed! Use a 15 cm (6 in) square of thin paper such as origami paper, airmail paper or undercopy (bank) typing paper. Heavier paper will not float the design through the air.

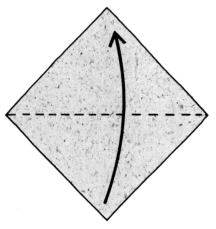

1 Fold in half along a diagonal.

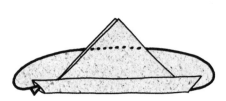

3 Tuck one end of the hem into the pocket at the other end, bending the paper into a circle with the hem on the outside.

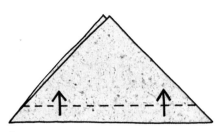

2 Fold up the lower edge a little way. Try to keep the crease exactly parallel to the edge.

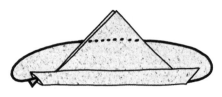

4 The Glider is complete. Make sure that the leading edge is a neat circle.

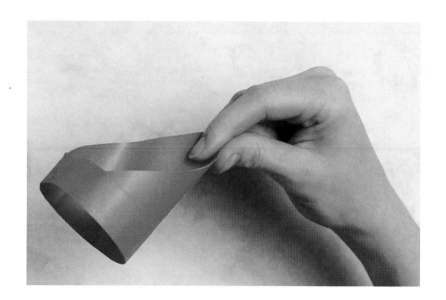

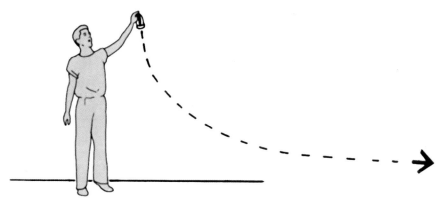

5 Hold as shown, high above your head, with the Glider pointing downwards. Release it gently. It will fall quickly at first, then level out and glide a considerable distance. Remember to release it gently. Never throw or push it.

SAMPAN

This design has a remarkable climax when, at Steps 10-12, the entire shape is turned inside-out to suddenly reveal the completed Sampan. A few other designs contain inversions to part of their structure, but none to this extent. A simpler variation is to regard Step 5 as a flat, uncreased square, then to proceed as diagrammed, but omitting Step 13 to create a boat without a canopy. Use a 15-20 cm (6-8 in) square of paper with different colours on the two sides. Begin by creasing both diagonals, then folding a pair of opposite corners to the middle.

1 Tuck the corners inside.

3 Fold the remaining corners to the centre.

2 Turn over.

4 Similarly, tuck these corners inside.

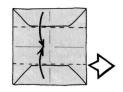

5 Fold the top and bottom edges to the centre.

6 Turn in the triangles.

7 Narrow one end, then . . .

8 . . . narrow the other.

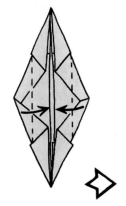

9 Fold the side corners to the centre.

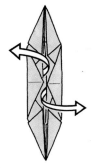

10 Pull the side layers right apart to expose a clean base . . .

11 . . . like this. Keep the layers pressed together. Turn over.

12 The arrowed corners point towards you. Push them down with considerable force, so that they invert backwards and the sampan turns inside-out . . .

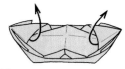

13 . . . like this. Lift up the canopies.

14 The Sampan is complete.

JUNK

The sequence of folds to make the Junk is regarded by many as the most beautiful in all origami, particularly the transformations in Step 2, Steps 5-7, Steps 13-15 and Steps 19-20. Note how the sequence progresses effortlessly from one step to the next like notes in a melody or steps in a ballet, topped by the final extraordinary opening out climax. Use a 15-20 cm (6-8 in) square of paper with different colours on the two sides. Begin with Step 1 of the Sampan (see page 26).

1 Note A and B. Turn over.

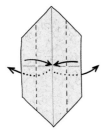

2 Fold the sides to the centre, so that A and B flip to the front . . .

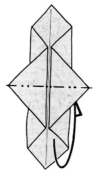

3 . . . like this. Mountain fold the lower portion behind.

4 Pre-crease as shown, through all layers.

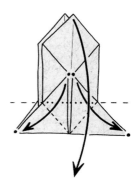

5 Fold dot to dot, left and right. This will open the slit down the centre and swivel C downward by a considerable distance.

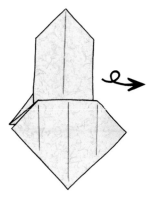

6 Note the position of C. Turn over.

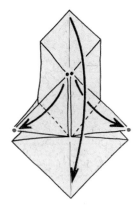

7 Repeat 4-6 with D.

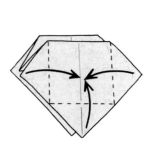

8 Fold the corners to the centre. Repeat behind.

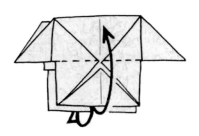

9 Fold the lower edge up to the top. Repeat behind.

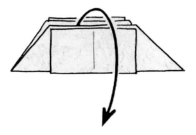

10 Pull down the front two layers.

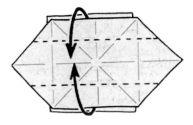

11 Narrow the top layer.

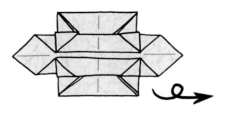

12 Turn over.

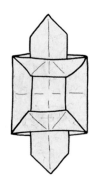

15 The result is this picture frame, or intriguing belt and buckle illusion. Turn over.

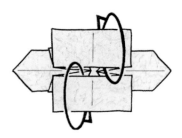

13 Swivel the top flaps around to the back . . .

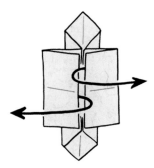

16 Fold out the side flaps.

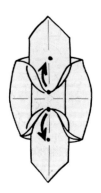

14 . . . like this. The paper is now 3D, so flatten it by folding dot, dot.

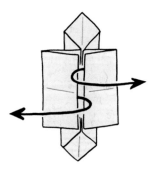

17 On trhe left, fold in the edge. On the right, unfold the triangle.

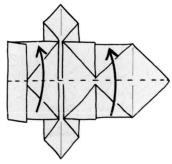

18 Fold in half, as seen on the right.

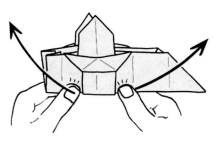

19 Hold tightly as shown on the left. Pull the paper outwards then upwards, so that the inner layers inside the 'belt' are unrolled into view.

20 The junk is completed. Strenghten all the creases.

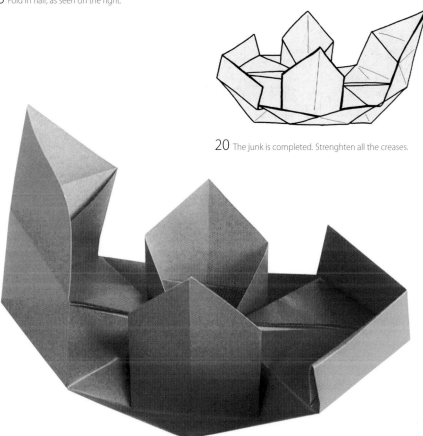

EASTERN DESIGNS

Origami is the Japanese word for 'paper-folding' and is used around the world as a tribute to the original home of the art, some 1500 years ago. The best contemporary designs reveal qualities typical of oriental arts and crafts – elegance, stylization and, in designs of living creatures, more regard for character than for form. The wide range of beautiful papers (the country is renowned for its papers). often mean that more attention is given to the look of a design than to its sequence of folds, so that the artistry lies more in the relationships between the paper, the subject and the manipulative finesse of the folder, than in the ballet of the sequence. These designs

particularly those of living creatures by the greatest of origami masters, Akira Yoshizawa – are uncannily alive, but are almost unreproduceable by we lesser folders who do not have 'the spirit'. Fortunately, though, for books such as this, there is a large body of work that can be reproduced by the lay folder in conventional papers.

In recent years, a less emotive, more geometric style of folding has emerged, drawing not a little inspiration from the technological advances made in the West since the 1950s. The Cube and Stretch Wall are examples of this style.

Outside Japan, there are known to be creative folders in Hong Kong, Singapore and Malaysia.

YOSHIZAWA'S BUTTERFLIES

Akira Yoshizawa is the single most important paper-folder in the world. He was born in 1911, at a time when origami meant little more to the Japanese than the mechanical reproduction of a few traditional designs, and when creative origami was virtually unknown. As with many children, origami became an absorbing hobby of his. Unlike other children though, it later became such an obsession that at the age of 26 he left his job in an iron foundry (where he had usefully learnt the principles of geometry) to devote himself to origami. For a decade he worked alone and in poverty, inventing many new designs and forging his philosophy of creative origami. Shortly before World War II, a twist of fate brought him much publicity and an influential patron to guide him on his professional career.

After the war, Yoshizawa resumed his career, publishing his first book in 1952, establishing the International Origami Center in 1954 and first exhibiting in Europe in 1955. Since then, he has received many cultural honours and travelled widely, including several visits to the West where origami enthusiasts have acclaimed his work.

Yoshizawa separates origami into two kinds: 'recreational' and 'art'. The former he largely dismisses as being the mechanical reproduction of a design to give an illustrative likeness of a subject, but without expression or character. Such designs include all traditional and geometric work and almost all other modern creative work, from East or West. To Yoshizawa, these designs may be clever, but they are without spirit. He advocates an origami which reveals the inner character of the subject through the interpretive skills of the paper-folder. Mere symbolic representation is not enough: the folder must have an empathy for the subject he is folding and the material he uses (the paper). If this suggests a philosophy that is too all-embracing and too emotional to be practised by the reader who wishes his origami to simply be an enjoyable pastime,

then it is a measure of Yoshizawa's complete commitment to his art.

However total or controversial Yoshizawa's approach may be, there can be no doubting the quality of his work, the range and diversity of which is legendary. In particular, his finesse with paper is without equal. It is so exquisite as to defy reproduction by any other folder. Diagrams can only show the bare bones of a design, which the folder through dedicated practice must flesh out and bring to life.

The butterflies photographed here (which have all been folded by Yoshizawa and generously donated for use in the book) show a good cross-section of his work, from the very simple to the very complex, but all beautifully folded. The simpler ones can be folded by anybody, even young children. Although they are examples of the 'recreational' style which he does not usually support, they can be made to flutter when the central ridge is depressed, bringing them to life and so earning them a place in his renowned and charismatic teaching performances.

The more complex ones show his engineering prowess. Were this a Yoshizawa book, the designs would be yet more beautiful, but western writers are not usually permitted to publish the very best of his work. Indeed, visitors to his home-cum-studio in Tokyo say that the most extraordinary of his pieces remain unpublished.

It is possible to conceive that a modern origami movement would have evolved without Yoshizawa, but his genius has enriched the art for all time.

YOSHIZAWA'S BUTTERFLY

Here are the instructions for Yoshizawa's best-known Butterfly, drawn by the creator for use in the book and reproduced without alterations or additions. This butterfly is the logo of the International Origami Center, which Yoshizawa founded to help spread friendship and peace through origami. The design is so well-known that it has almost become traditional.

Yoshizawa does not give the written step by step instructions as we have done in other designs, but by now the reader should be familiar enough with the diagrams and symbols to be able to follow his instructions.

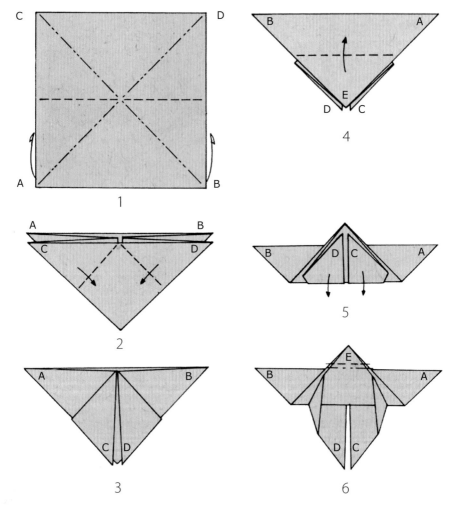

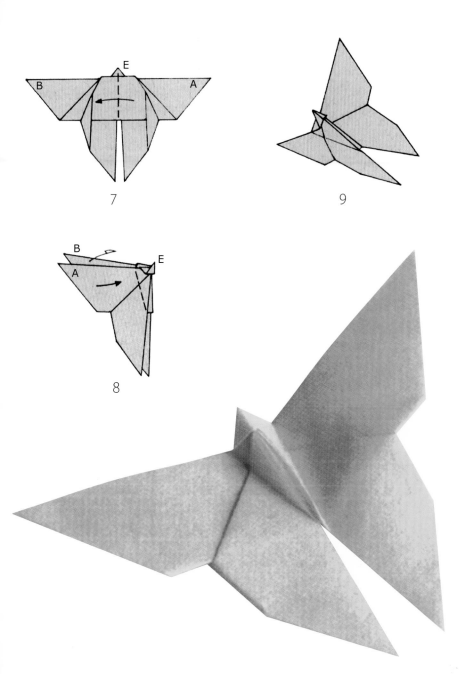

MOUNT FUJI AND THE SEA

The late creator of this design, Seiryo Takegawa (Japan), specialized in producing very simple designs for children, including many wonderful action toys. This little-known masterpiece is typical of his work: simple, poetic, audacious and charming. Perhaps it is like the traditional Bird on page 16 – more a symbol than a representation. Use a 15-20 cm (6-8 in) square. Origami paper is ideal.

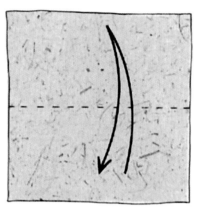

1 Fold in half. Unfold.

3 Mountain fold the top corners behind, so that the verticle edges are brought down level with the horizontal fold.

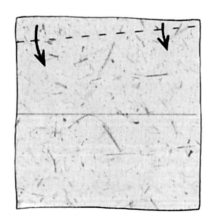

2 Fold down the top edge a little way, more on the left than on the right.

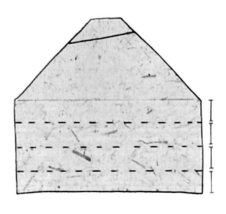

4 Divide the lower section into quarters. All the creases must be valleys.

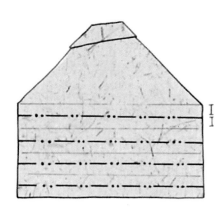

5 Place mountains between the valleys. Pleate the creases, including the original horizontal fold.

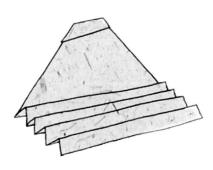

6 Mount Fuji and the Sea complete.

YACHT

There are many origami yachts, boats and ships, but none are as simple or as full of movement as this wonderful design by Japan's First Lady of origami, Mrs Toshie Takahama. Mrs Takahama has produced many exquisite designs, particularly of animals (see her Cat on page 54) and flowers. She has written several books, some of which have recently been translated into English. Use a 15-20 cm (6-8 in) square of origami paper.

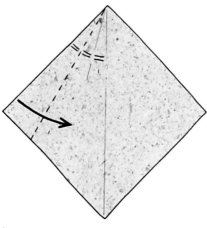

1 Fold in the top edge one third of the way towards the diognal crese.

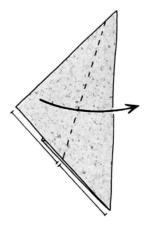

3 Fold it back along a crease which starts just to the left of the top corner and goes to the mid-point of the lower edge.

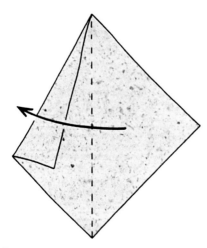

2 Fold the right hand corner across to the left.

4 Fold the bottom corner across to the right.

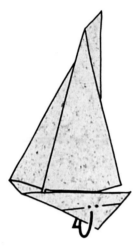

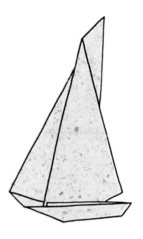

5 Mountain fold the bottom corner behind.

6 The Yacht complete.

ETERNALLY OPENING ORIGAMI

This design is Step 13 of the Flapping Bird (see page 28) turned upside down. It is nothing more than the classic Bird Base, familiar to all experienced folders. What makes it remarkable is that no one until Takuji Sugimura of Japan realized that it could perform the addictive dance described here. The lesson, of course, is never to disregard the familiar in case it holds a wonderful secret. Use a 15-20 cm (6-8 in) of paper.

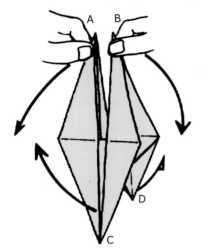

1 Hold points A and B. Separate your hands, moving them outwards and downwards, allowing C and D to rise . . .

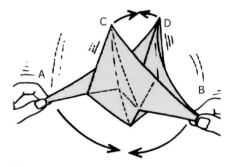

3 . . . like this. Continue until A and B are together at the bottom.

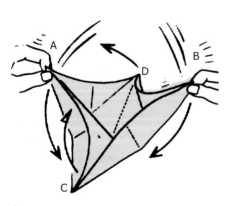

2 . . . like this. Begin to bring A and B back together below C and D . . .

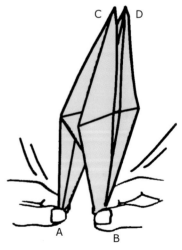

4 The movement complete. Strengthen the creases.

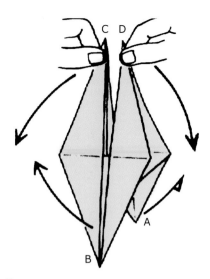

5 Transfer your hands to C and D and repeat Steps 1-4.

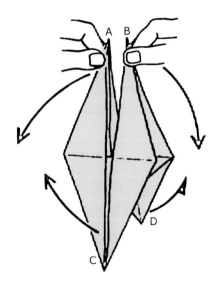

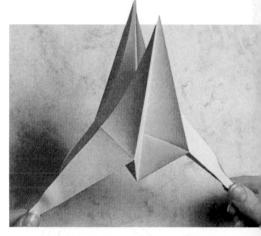

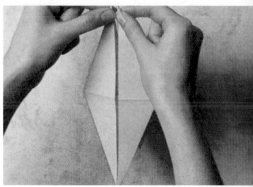

6 Transfer your hands back to A and B and repeat and repeat and repeat! Be careful at Step 2 not to pull A and B too far apart, or the paper will 'snap' and lock to look like Step 2 of the Daffodil stem on page 88.

CUBE

The creator of the Cube, Shuzo Fujimoto (Japan) has conducted a great deal of research into the geometry of folding, including important discoveries about how to fold accurate polygons (pentagons, hexagons, and so on) from a square; how to divide an edge into accurate thirds, fifths, etc without 'guesstimating'; and how to fold a one-piece solid such as a tetrahedron or an icosahedron. If all this sounds rather dry (it isn't!), just enjoy folding his Cube. In particular, enjoy Step 5 – surely one of the 'best moves' in all origami. Use a 15-20 cm (6-8 in) square of thin or medium weight paper.

1 Carefully divide the paper into quarters. horizontally and vertically, to create 16 squares.

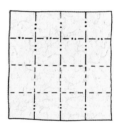

2 Re-crease the creases to look like the pattern of mountains and valleys shown here.

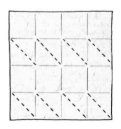

3 Add eight short diagonals. Be precise.

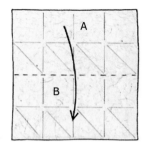

4 Fold in half. Note squares A and B.

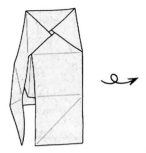

7 Turn over.

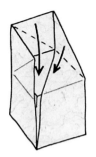

10 Push in the next corner . . .

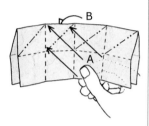

5 Hold as shown. Note square A at the front and B behind. The aim is now to slide A up and to the left so that it exactly covers B. When this has happened, the paper will have curled into a cube form. All of the marked creases must form cleanly and simultaneously. There is a knack to this 'slide', so please try it several times.

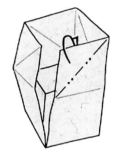

8 Fold in the corner.

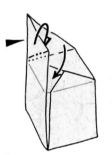

11 . . . and the next.

12 Tuck the triangle inside the cube to lock the top.

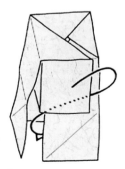

6 Tuck the front square inside to lock the top.

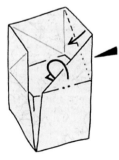

9 Push in the next corner to form part of the lid.

13 The cube completed.

CAT

This is another design by Mrs Toshie Takahama (see also her Yacht on page 36). The cat is regarded by many creative folders to be a very difficult subject to capture in paper, because its shape is very simple and curved. In the opinion of the author, Mrs Takahama's Cat is the most successful version yet achieved, being well proportioned, full of character, instantly recognizeable and pleasing to fold. The design benefits from being made from a textured paper such as Ingres (Strathmore), or another appropriate paper. Begin with Step 3 of the Bird (see page 20), using a 15-20 cm (6-8 in) square of paper as in that design.

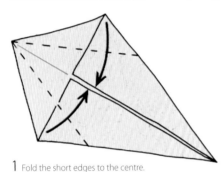

1 Fold the short edges to the centre.

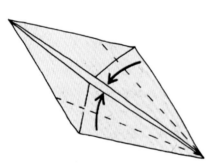

2 Narrow the corner at the right. Keep the corner as neat as possible.

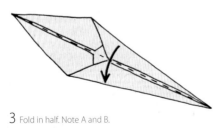

3 Fold in half. Note A and B.

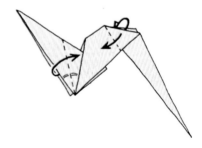

4 Reverse the blunt corner along AB, then ...

5 ... reverse it back up level with open edge. Reverse the sharp corner to the position shown in Step 6.

6 Valley the front layer at the left across to the right, so that the point stands upright. Turn the sharp point inside out.

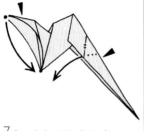

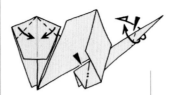

7 Squash the point, dot to dot. Reverse the tail.

9 Fold the ears forward. Reverse the hind legs. Outside reverse the tail.

11 Fold up the ears.

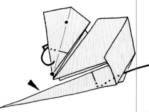

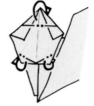

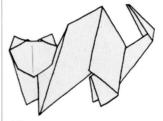

8 Tuck the point inside the face, folding dot to dot. Reverse the tail.

10 Shape the nose. Fold the top of the head behind.

12 The Cat complete.

INCENSE BURNER

The Reverend Philip Shen (Hong Kong) specializes in creating geometric designs which collapse into shape from a carefully laid out pattern of pre-creases. The Incense Burner is one of his finest designs, particularly because the final shape is conjoured from a very familiar pattern of pre-creases – the kite shape in Step 2 is known to all paper-folders, yet simply to repeat it on each corner and add the central star shape is enough to create a beautiful design. Use a 15-20 cm (6-10 in) square of medium weight paper.

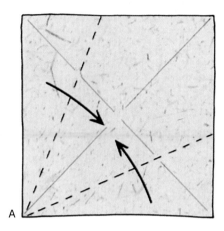

1 Fold the two edges meeting at A to the centre crease.

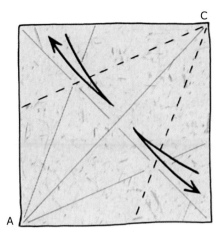

3 Repeat with the other two edges meeting at C.

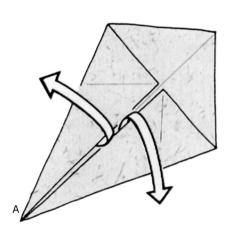

2 Unfold.

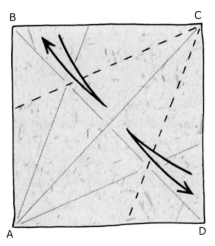

4 Repeat with the two edges meeting at B, then those meeting at D.

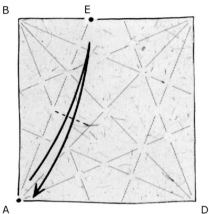

5 Fold A to E, E being at the end of the upper crease made in Step 1. Crease only where shown.

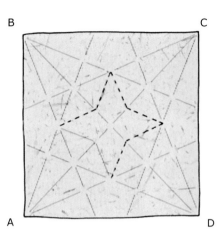

7 Repeat with B C and D, making 6 more short creases.

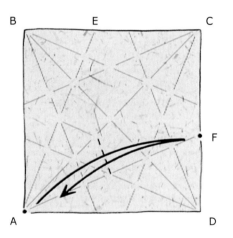

6 Repeat, folding A to F, F being at the end of the lower crease made in Step 1.

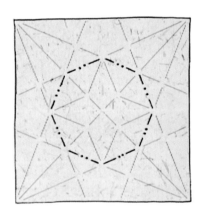

8 Re-crease the octagon with mountain creases.

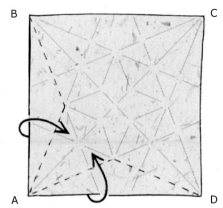

9 Fold in the creases as shown.

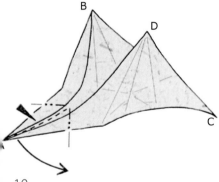

10 Reverse A along exisisting creases...

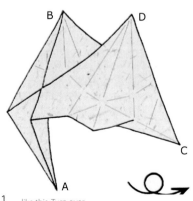

11 ...like this. Turn over.

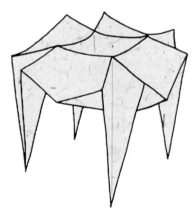

12 Strengthen the inner star shape with mountain creases. Turn back over and repeat Steps 9-11 with B C and D, forming three more legs.

13 The Incense Burner complete.

TULIP AND STEM

Here is the first two-piece design in the book and one of the simplest and most appealing of all origami flowers. Its creator, Kunihiko Kasahara (Japan), has written over 100 origami books – including some in English – which feature his own prolific output. To make the Tulip and Stem, make the Tulip square half the size of the Stem square, so that (for example) if the Tulip is made from a 10 cm (4 in) square, the Stem is made from an 20 cm (8 in) square. The Tulip begins with Step 6 of the Flapping Bird (see page 28) turned upside down and the Stem begins with Step 3 of the Bird (see page 20).

BLOOM

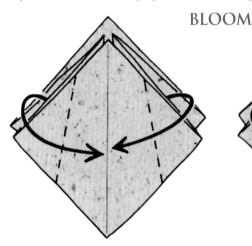

1 With the open corner at the top, fold the front corners to the centre crease. Note that the creases taper towards the top. Repeat behind.

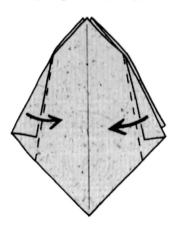

3 Fold the open edges to the crease. Repeat behind.

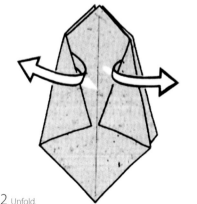

2 Unfold.

4 Fold over along Step 1 creases. Repeat behind.

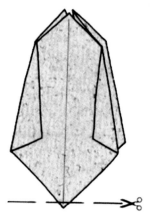

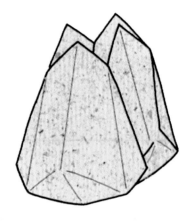

5 With a pair of scissors, snip off the tip. Snip off less than you think you should – the hole can be enlarged with another snip, but cannot be made smaller!

7 The Bloom complete.

6 Open out.

STEM

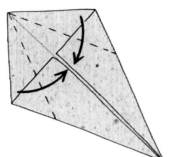

1 Fold the short edges to the centre crease.

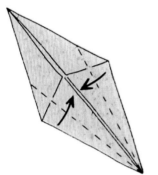

2 Narrow the bottom corner. Keep it neat.

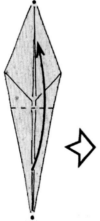

3 Fold in half, dot to dot.

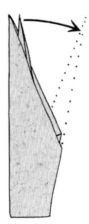

4 Pull the sharp point out to the dotted position. Squeeze the paper flat at the bottom to let the sharp point retain its new position.

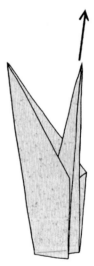

5 The Stem complete. Insert the sharp spike into the base of the Bloom.

FOX

The stylization typical of Japanese designs is shown to good effect in this design by Mitsue Okuda. What's more, although the front and back are folded differently (the tail is to one side), the design looks good from all angles.

The head is a particularly interesting feature of the design, being so remarkably simple. Use an oblong of thin or medium weight paper, twice as long as it is wide, for instance 10-20 cm (4-8 in).

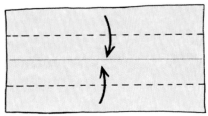

1 Fold the long edges to the centre crease.

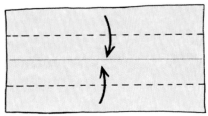

2 Reverse twice at the left.

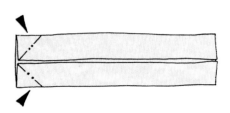

3 Mountain fold in half.

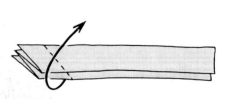

4 Valley fold.

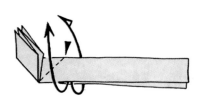

5 Outside reverse.

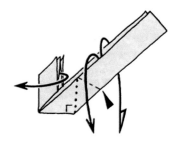

6 Pull two layers across to the left to allow the centre point (the nose) to rise. Outside reverse on the right, as shown.

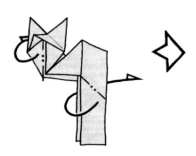

7 Mountain the tail. Fold the left ear around the back.

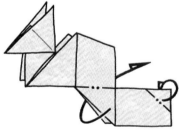

8 Narrow the tip of the tail. Mountain fold the tail behind.

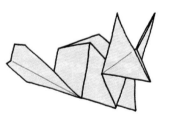

10 The Fox complete.

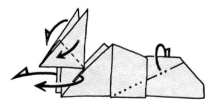

9 Narrow the tail. Pull the ears forward.

STRETCH WALL

The basic grid made in Step 6 can, with the addition of diagonal creases, be collapsed into any number of geometric patterns, some very complex. This design by Yoshihide Momotani of Japan is one of the most astonishing, being elastic – that is, it can expand and collapse. Also, whereas the front is a horizontal pattern of bricks,

the reverse shows the same pattern, but vertically! The design is not difficult, but time-consuming. Fold the grid very carefully and the later folds will fall into place. The final 'unpicking' of the edges in Steps 18-20 is a very pretty and dramatic conclusion. Use a sheet of thin or medium weight paper at least 20 cm (8 in) square.

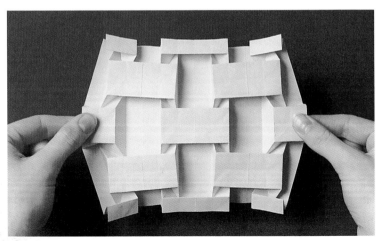

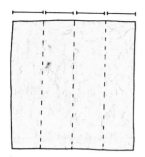

1 Crease accurate quarters, all valleys.

4 Check that the top crease is a valley (if it isn't, turn the paper over so that it is).

7 Make pleats where shown . . .

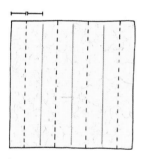

2 Crease accurate eighths, all valleys.

5 Repeat Steps 1-3, creasing valleys as quarters and eighths, then mountains in between . . .

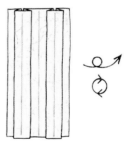

8 . . . like this. Turn the paper over and rotate.

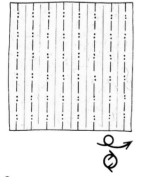

3 Place mountains midway between the valleys. Turn over and rotate the paper.

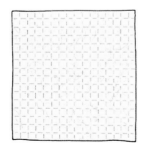

6 . . .to make this grid.

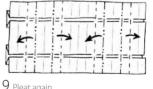

9 Pleat again.

10 The pleats complete. Note A B and C. Fold dot to dot, so that the lower pleat swivels downwards . . .

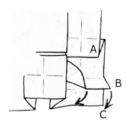

11 . . . like this. Note the diagonal crease which has to be made beneath the vertical pleat to accommodate the swivel.

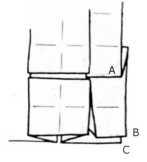

12 The swivel and hidden diognal creases complete.

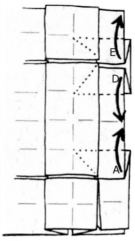

13 Repeat the swivel with A D and E.

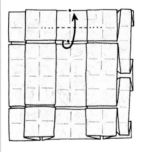

14 Repeat down centre, swivelling the pleat upwards to lie level with the top edge.

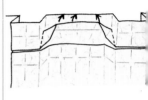

15 As before, diagonal creases need to be made beneath the vertical pleats, this time one at each end of the swivel.

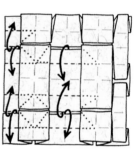

16 The swivel complete. Repeat three more times down the centre, then four times down the left hand edge.

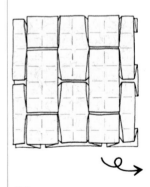

17 The swivels complete. Turn over.

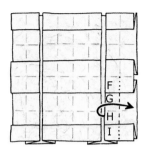

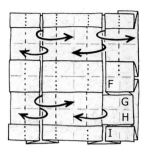

18 Note FG and HI. Fold edge GH across to the right, so that G separates from F and H separates from I . .

20 . . . like this. Repeat, unbuttoning more edges to reveal a regular brick pattern.

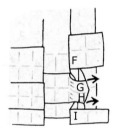

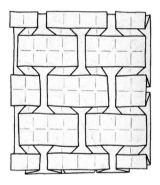

19 . . . like this. Pull out the paper beneath F and I, so that edge GH can flatten to the right . . .

21 The Stretch Wall complete. Hold opposite edges and pull apart to open the bricks.

WESTERN DESIGNS

Creative origami in the West – as a creative movement, at least – began in the 1950s. A surprising number of traditional designs were known before that time, such as the triangular newspaper hat and the paper dart, but the creative potential of the art had not been explored to any depth. In the 1950s, a few key books, exhibitions and TV programmes established the art, since when it has continued to grow and diversify, perhaps by now surpassing even the Japanese for innovation.

There are now many styles of folding, created by enthusiasts who fold for many reasons: for some it is a decorative craft, or perhaps a form of puzzle solving, for others it is an exploration of geometry, a way to relax, an aid to teaching or simply because the possibility of folding a sheet of paper into a recognizable form is an extraordinary phenomenon.

The designs in this chapter show the preoccupation of most western creative folders with engineering and geometry, rather than the artistry of the eastern designers. These designs are complex (some fearsomely so) but for reasons of space, few are included here. Instead, the chapter presents some of the simpler classics. For those who would like to fold complex designs, many can be found in books published in the United States by Engel, Montroll, Lang and Weiss.

ARROW

Some designs are so simple and seemingly so obvious that they appear to have been 'discovered', rather than 'created'. It is almost as though they were there all the time. To see these designs in the paper demands an original approach, not just a reworking of familiar techniques. This design by Tun Ken Lamb (England) may not be to your taste, but its originality is startling. Use a square of paper of any size differently coloured on the two sides.

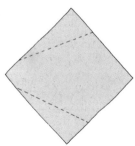

1 Fold in the top and bottom corners to the position shown in Step 2.

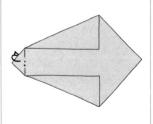

2 Turn back the corner triangle.

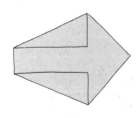

3 Turn Arrow complete.

SNAP HEXAHEDRON

Hexahedrons are common in origami. This one by Edwin Corrie (England) is one of the simplest and features an interesting move at Step 5. To make the 3 x 3 grid of squares needed in Step 1, fold a 4 x 4 grid by creasing halves and quarters horizontally and vertically, then cut off a line of squares along two adjacent edges to leave a 3 x 3 grid. Use a 15 cm (6 in) square of paper. Large squares will not 'snap' at Step 7.

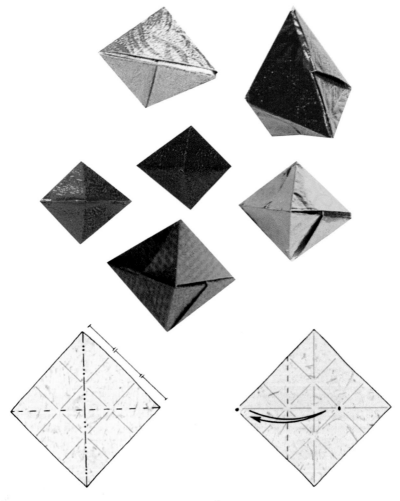

1 Fold the vertical diagonal as a mountain and the horizontal diagonal as a valley.

2 Fold dot to dot. Unfold.

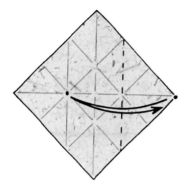

3 Similarly, fold dot to dot. Unfold.

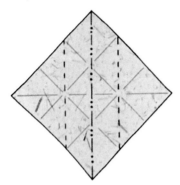

4 Pleat as shown.

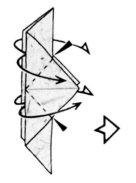

5 Outside reverse the top and bottom corners.

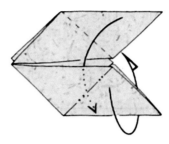

6 Valley fold the top corner into the pocket formed by the lower outside reverse fold. Then, mountain the lower corner into the upper outside reverse fold, behind.

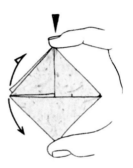

7 Hold as shown and squeeze. The left hand corners will separate to create a third edge around the middle, forming a 3D hexahedron.

8 The Snap Hexahedron complete.

UN-UNFOLDABLE BOX

Boxes are the most common subject in origami. Some are very complex and ornate, whereas this one by Ed Sullivan (USA) is particularly plain. However, the fascination of this design is in the folding, because once folded, it cannot then be unfolded, at least not without making extra folds or fumbling with the paper. It is unique in origami and a remarkable design. Use a large square of medium weight paper.

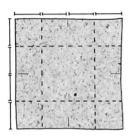

1 Pinch the mid-points of the four edges. Use them as a guide to make four valley creases along the horizontal and vertical quarter marks. Pinch the mid-points of the four edges. Use them as a guide to make four valley creases along the horizontal and vertical quarter marks.

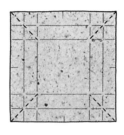

3 Form valley diagonals at the corners, to create a box with triangular flaps.

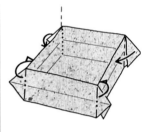

5 Fold the triangles to the inside, flat against the box.

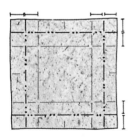

2 Make mountain folds midway between the valley quarters and the edges.

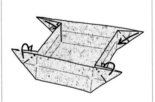

4 Point two flaps to the left and two to the right. Fold the triangles in half by turning the loose corners inside.

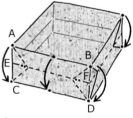

6 Collapse, bringing A down to C and B down to D. E and F move towards the centre of the front edge. Repeat behind.

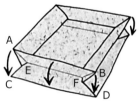

7 This is the shape half collapsed...

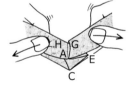

9 Hold corner AC as shown. Pull your hands gently apart and H will slide away from G...

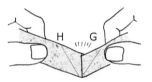

11 ...until the corner is fully formed. Repeat at the other corners of the box.

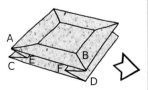

8 ...and here fully collapsed. Note E and F.

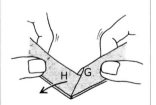

10 ...like this. Keep pulling...

12 The Un-unfoldable Box complete.

FACE

Many liberties can be taken with the shape of a face before it becomes unrecognizable, which is why origami faces are a particular interesting subject for creative paper folders. Not all the facial features need be present. This face by Steven Casey (Australia) for example does not have a mouth. Other designs may only have a nose, or just the hair, or may be extraordinarily detailed, even sculpted-looking. The shapes for this face are strong and harmonious, and the sequence is clean and flowing. Use a 15-20 cm (6-8 in) square. paper with different colours on the two sides

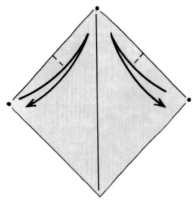

1 Fold the top corner to the left and right corners in turn, pinching the mid points of the top edges.

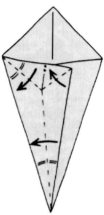

3 Make creases to bisect each of the three angles on the triangular flap, so that the flap collapses to look like Step 4. Repeat on the right.

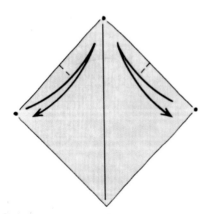

2 Make creases which connect each mid-point with the bottom corner, folding the left and right corners across the middle.

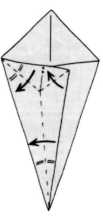

4 Turn the loose flaps inside-out, so that they change colour.

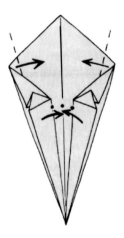

5 Swivel the triangles inwards so that they meet at the centre.

7 Repeat on the left.

6 Fold over.

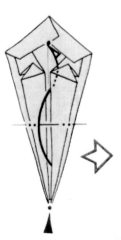

8 Reverse (or sink) the bottom point up inside the face, turning the point inside out.

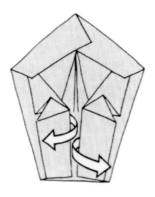

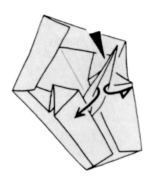

9 Pull the cheeks apart to expose the point just reversed.

11 ... like this. Squash it flat.

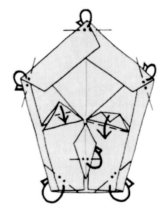

10 Form three creases as shown to make the point stand upright…

12 On the left, fold down the loose point of the eye to look like the eye drawn on the other side of the face, then fold it downwards. Blunt the nose. Round off the chin and hair.

13 The Face complete.

ROOSTER

This design by Florence Temko (USA) is a superb example of how a few carefully placed inside and outside reverse folds can create a design with style and character from the very familiar origami shape shown in Step 6 (sometimes called a Fish Base). The design when folded looks folded, which, curiously, not all origami does. A design which has clearly been folded without the need to cut or fold pieces together is somehow more satisfying. Use a 15-20 cm (6-8 in) square of medium weight paper. Crease and unfold both diagonals.

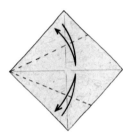

1 Fold the bottom left and top left edges to the centre crease. Unfold.

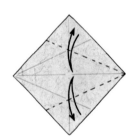

2 Repeat on the right.

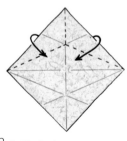

3 Fold in the three creases as shown, so that the top corner stands upright . . .

4 . . . like this. Flatten it to the left.

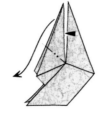

8 Reverse.

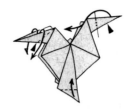

11 At the left, outside reverse. At the right, reverse. Valley the feet. Repeat behind. The valley creases on the feet should be at such an angle that the Rooster can balance.

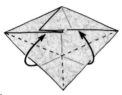

5 Repeat at the bottom, once more flattening the loose corner to the left.

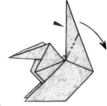

9 Reverse. Note the angle

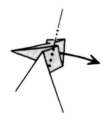

12 Reverse the beak

6 Mountain the bottom portion behind.

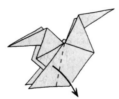

10 Valley, repeat behind.

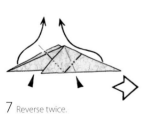

7 Reverse twice.

13 The Rooster complete.

POP-UP DOUBLE CUBE

The late and much missed Eric Kenneway (England) specialized in creating designs which were marvellous to fold but which when complete, did not always look too spectacular. For him, the joy of origami was in the folding, not the looking. His Pop-up Double Cube is perhaps an extreme example of his thesis – it has a fine sequence with intriguing moves at Steps 4-6, Step 11 and the climactic opening at Step 16, but the result looks very ordinary. Of its kind, it is a masterpiece. Use a 15-20 cm (6-8 in) square of medium weight paper.

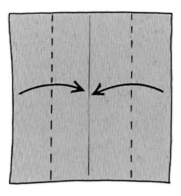

1 Valley the edges to the centre crease.

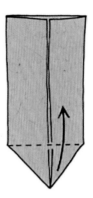

3 Fold up the triangle.

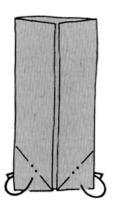

2 Mountain the bottom corners behind.

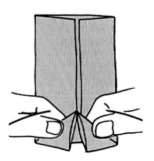

4 Moisten your fingers for a good grip and hold as shown. Pull the outer layers, sliding them out to the sides . . .

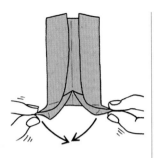

5 ... like this. Flatten the paper by bringing the corners together.

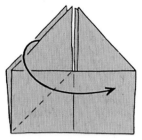

8 Fold across to the right

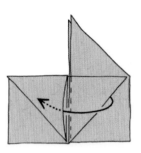

11 Tuck the loose triangle right into the pocket. Keep it neat.

6 The move complete. Repeat Steps 2–6 at the top.

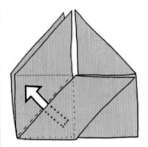

9 Pull out the hidden corner.

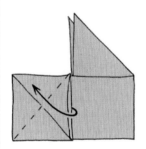

12 Fold the loose corner up and to the left.

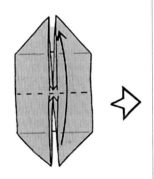

7 Fold in half.

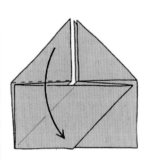

10 Fold down the triangle.

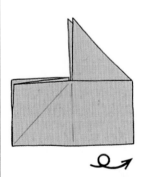

13 The left side is complete. Turn over.

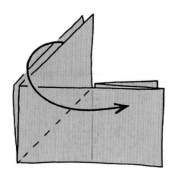

14 Repeat Steps 7-13 on this side.

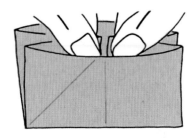

16 Hold as shown and pull the central flaps upwards and outwards . . .

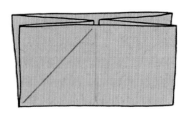

15 Creasing complete.

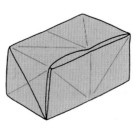

17 . . . like this, to form the completed Pop-up Double Cube.

STAR

Origami, like all arts and crafts, is prone to trends. The latest is 'modular' folding, in which identical units are folded and inter – locked to form flat patterns, solids or stars. Some of these systems are very beautiful, perhaps profound. This Star by Nick Robinson (England) is very simple and particularly elegant in its construction. It need not have 5 points – any number greater than 2 will interlock. For a Star, use at least five sheets of square paper, either all the same colour or all different, depending on your taste. A 7.5 cm (3 in) square is good size.

MODULE

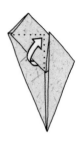

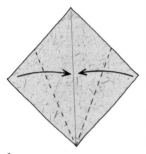

1 Fold the lower edges to the centre crease.

3 Repeat, but now with the opposite edge.

5 Pull out A to the front.

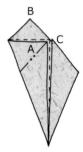

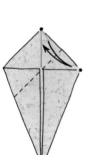

2 Fold dot to dot, as shown.

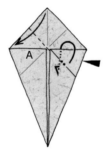

4 Re-fold Step 3, but this time reverse folding the lower right portion of the crease. Note A.

6 Crease two valleys and a mountain as shown, to give the module some shape …

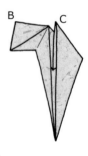

7 … like this. The module is complete. For a Star, make four more.

ASSEMBLY

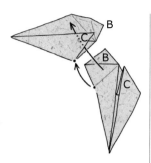
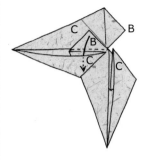
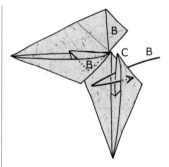

1 Hold two modules as shown. Note points B and C. Slide B on the lower module under C on the top module, bringing the two dots together …

2 … like this. Tuck B into the pocket at C.

3 Repeat the locking pattern, locking another B into the C pocket. Continue, locking the fifth module into the first to close the sequence of locks and complete the Star. Strengthen all creases.

4 The Star complete.

DAFFODIL

Technically, this design by Ted Norminton (England) is the most advanced in the book and should only be attempted by experienced folders. Compare it with the much simpler Tulip and Stem on page 60 – the two extremes of style show how beauty can be achieved by very different means. Note the intriguing method in Steps 1-6 for folding an accurate hexagon. Persevere with the difficult 'sink' at Step 11 – practice will make it much easier. Use a medium weight yellow square for the bloom and a green square of the same size for the stem. A 25 cm (10 in) square will create a life-size bloom.

BLOOM

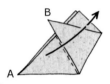

3 Fold the left corner across.

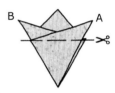

4 Cut off the upper portion of paper as shown.

5 Open out …

6 … to reveal a perfect hexagon! Crease mountains and valleys as shown, collapsing them to make Step 7.

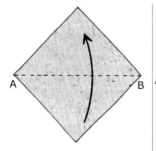

1 Fold in half along a diagonal.

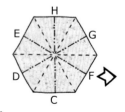

2 Pinch the mid-point and the upper quarter point. Fold the mid point edge on to the quarter point crease, so that the new crease runs exactly to the centre of the bottom edge. Be very accurate.

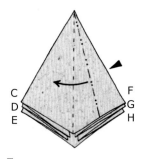

7 If the bottom edge runs straight across, turn the whole shape inside-out to make the shape seen here. Lift F and squash . . .

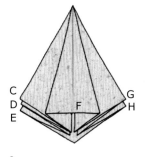

8 . . . like this. Repeat with C D E G and H. When squashing, try to keep the same number of layers left and right.

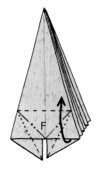

9 Lift point F along the marked creases (petal fold).

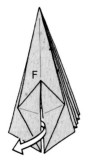

10 Unfold the Step 9 creases. Repeat five more times.

11 Invert or sink the top corner down into the body of the paper, at the level shown. Open out the. hexagon to do so, then collapse it back into shape when the rim of the sink has been creased into a continuous mountain crease and the centre inverted. This is a difficult and lengthy procedure, even for experts, so persevere.

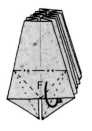

12 Tuck F up inside the front layer, reversing some of the Step 9 creases. Repeat five more times around the layers.

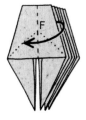

13 Fold one layer across to the left, to reveal . . .

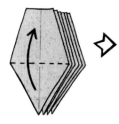

14 . . . a clean face. Fold up the bottom triangle. Repeat five more times around the layers.

15 Fold one layer across . . .

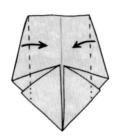

18 Re-fold the Step 16 creases, so that the bottom portion of each crease disappears into the lower triangle.

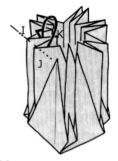

20 Note I J and K again. Fold K behind, so that I and J are brought together and locked. Repeat five more times within the Bloom.

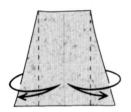

16 . . . to reveal a clean face. Note that for clarity, only the front layer will now be drawn. Crease and unfold as shown.

19 Fold the layer across. Repeat Steps 15-19 five more times. Note I J and K.

21 Pull down each of the six petals and reverse the rim of the Bloom to shape it.

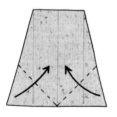

17 Fold the corners up to the centre crease.

22 The Bloom complete.

STEM

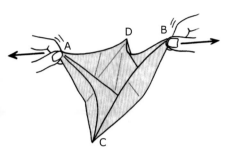

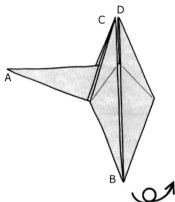

1 Begin with Step 2 of Eternally Opening Origami on page 50. Hold as shown. Pull A and B smartly apart, until the diagonal which connects them pops into a rigid mountain crease …

4 Note the position of B. Turn over.

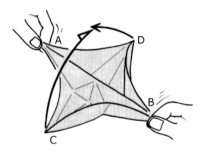

2 … like this. Flatten bringing C and D together.

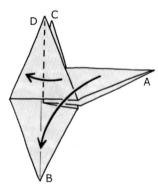

5 Repeat Step 3, swivelling A down to B.

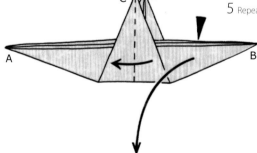

3 Fold the triangle in half below C, swivelling B downwards.

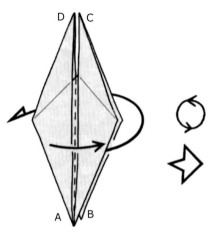

6 Fold a layer across at the front. Repeat behind but on the opposite side. Rotate the paper upside – down.

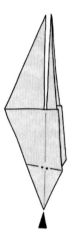

8 Push in or sink the bottom corner. Note that the crease tilts upward at the left. Repeat behind.

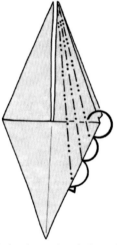

7 Narrow the front layer at the right. Repeat behind.

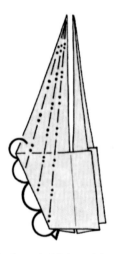

9 Narrow the flap on the left. Repeat behind.

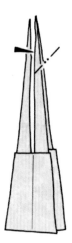

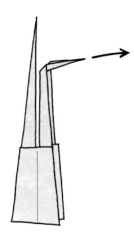

10 Reverse.

11 The Stem complete. Insert the spike into the back of the Bloom.

ARCHITECTURAL MODULE

This is not strictly a 'modular' design like the Star on page 86, because here there could be several different modules that lock together. The system is very much like a set of children's building blocks, which can be put together in many ways. Make as many as you can, then experiment with them to see what you can make – the photo shows just a few of the possibilities. The system is by Didier Boursin (France). Use squares of medium weight paper. 10 cm (4 in) squares will work well.

BAR MODULE: END LOCK

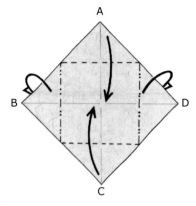

1 Valley corners A and C to the centre. Mountain corners B and D behind to the centre.

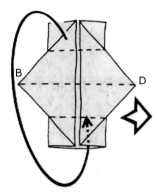

3 Crease three valleys as shown. Tuck the top edge deep inside the pocket at the bottom, locking the module into triangular shape.

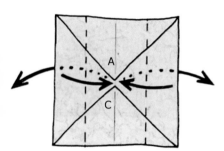

2 Fold the edges to the centre crease, allowing corners B and D to flip to the front.

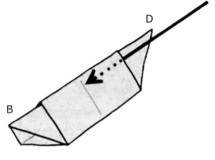

4 The completed module. The protruding triangles can lock into other modules …

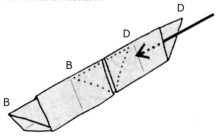

5 … like this. The chain can be extended infinitely.

BAR MODULE: SIDE LOCK

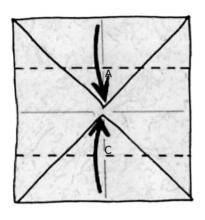

1 Begin with Step 2 above. Fold the top and bottom edges to the centre crease.

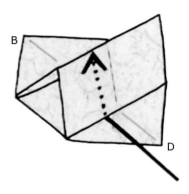

3 The completed module. The protruding triangles can tuck into other modules ...

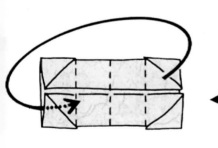

2 Crease three valleys. Tuck the right hand edge deep inside the pocket at the left edge, locking the module into a triangular shape. Allow corners B and D to flip out.

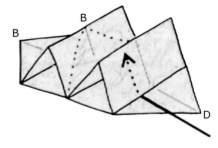

4 ... like this. The chain can be extended infinitely.

BAR MODULE: END AND SIDE LOCKS

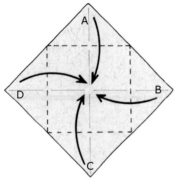

1 Fold the four corners to the middle.

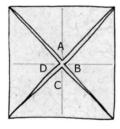

2 Turn over.

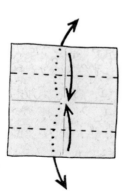

3 Fold the top and bottom edges to the centre crease, allowing corners A and C to flip out.

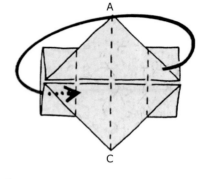

4 Crease three valleys as shown. Tuck the right edge deep into the pocket to lock the module into a triangular shape.

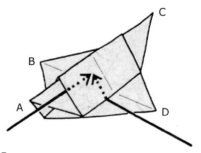

5 The module complete. Other modules can interlock at either end or either side, or both.

FOUR WAY JUNCTION

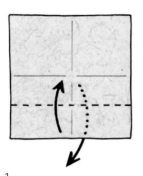

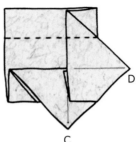

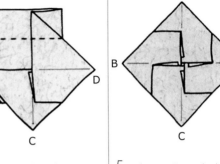

1 Begin with Step 3 of the End and Side Locks module above. Fold the bottom edge to the centre crease, allowing C to flip to the front.

3 Fold the top edge to the centre, allowing A to flip to the front.

5 ... the paper is completely symmetrical around the centre point. Turn over.

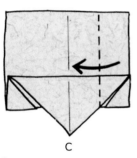

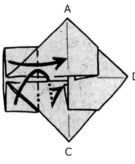

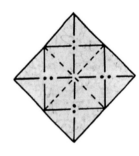

2 Fold the right edge to the centre, allowing D to flip to the front.

4 Fold the left edge to the centre, allowing B to flip to the front. Reverse the bottom section of the crease, so that ...

6 Crease and unfold mountains and valleys as shown, allowing the centre to rise towards you.

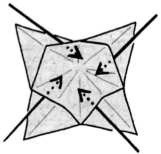

7 The completed module. Each protruding module can interlock with an End Lock module or Corner Junction (below).

CORNER JUNCTION

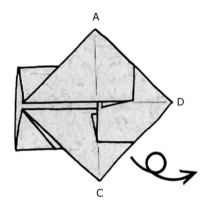

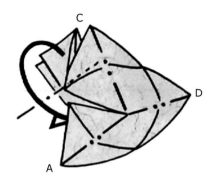

1 Begin with Step 4 of the Four-way Junction module. Turn over.

3 Fold the loose square inside the pyramid. Strengthen the creases which run from the apex to corners A C and D.

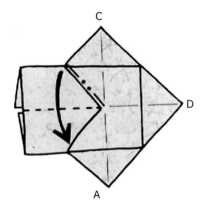

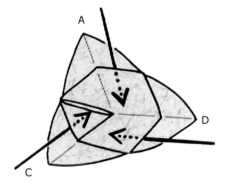

2 Form valley and mountain creases as shown, to make the shape 3D. The centre should rise towards you.

4 The completed module. Each protruding triangle can interlock with an End Lock module or a Four-way Junction.

BARKING DOG

An author should not perhaps include his own work in a book of classic origami, but I have to say that this design gives me great satisfaction. I discovered the action at Step 5 quite by accident whilst playing with the paper and looking for ways to resolve the shape into an acceptable design. From there, the head and tail just folded themselves. Use a 15-20 cm (6-8 in) square of thin or medium weight paper, differently coloured on the two sides. Start at Step 3 of the Bird on page 20.

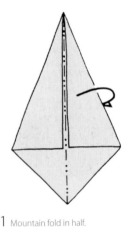

1 Mountain fold in half.

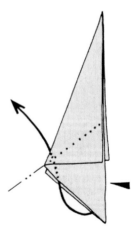

2 Reverse fold, to the position shown in Step 3.

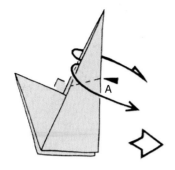

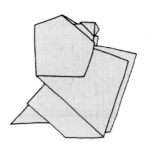

3 Outside reverse fold, to the position shown in Step 4. Note A.

6 Outside reverse fold, to the position shown in Step 4. Note A.

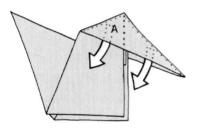

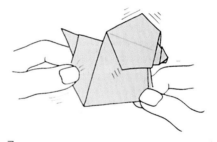

4 Full out the internal layer at A . . .

7 To make it bark, hold as shown and move your left hand to the left and back. The head will move up and down, as though barking!

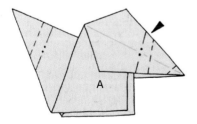

5 . . . like this. Repeat behind. Make three reverse folds on the head (the exact placement is unimportant). Pleat the tail.

ROWING BOAT

This design by Martin Wall (England) shows an elegant and concise way to create a simple shape. Steps 8-9 are particularly pleasing moves, not just for the way that they lock the boat into shape, but for the way in which the inside is kept clean. Made from metallic kitchen foil or greaseproof paper it will float. Otherwise, use a 15-20 cm (6-8 in) square of medium weight paper.

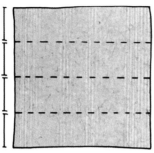

1 Valley into quarters.

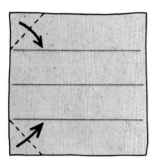

2 Turn in the left hand corners, top and bottom.

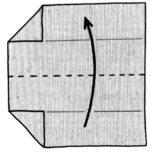

3 Fold in half.

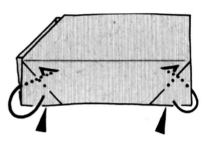

4 Reverse the bottom corners, level with the quarter crease.

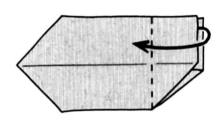

5 Open the reverse.

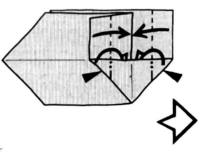

6 Reverse twice . . .

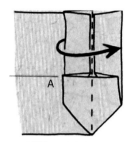

7 ... like this. Fold A across to the right.

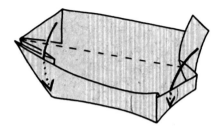

9 ... like this. Similarly, fold in the far side layer, but this time also folding it over the reverse at the bow to close it shut. Flatten the bottom of the boat.

8 Tuck the nearside top quarter into the boat. Take it over the top of A, but not over the top of the reverse fold layers at the bow (front) ...

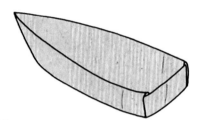

10 The Rowing Boat complete.

ROSETTE

Another design by the author. The idea is a development from a known fan lock, but here done twice between Steps 7-10, once either side of the centre. The result is Step 11, which was then found to 'snap' open obligingly to hold a satisfying circular shape under tension. For storage it can be collapsed flat back to Step 10! Use an oblong of medium weight paper, twice as long as is wide – for instance 10 x 20 cm (4 x 8 in).

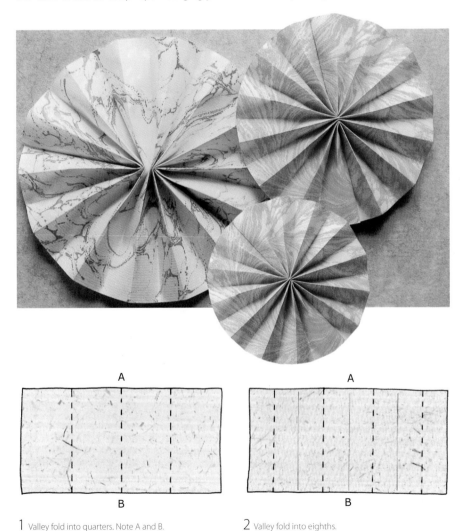

A

B

1 Valley fold into quarters. Note A and B.

A

B

2 Valley fold into eighths.

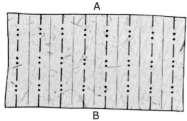

3 Place mountains between the valleys, so that ...

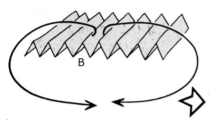

4 ...the folds concertina together. Unfold the central crease AB.

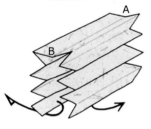

5 Unfold the first crease at each end of the pleats...

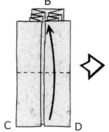

7 Fold in half. Note CD.

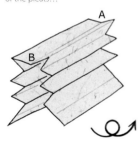

6 ... like this. Squash the pleats flat. Turn over.

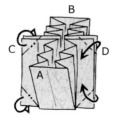

8 Allow the pleats to cascade open between A and B, but hold the central layers flat at C and D. At the right, turn in the corners with valley folds. At the left, do the same, but with mountain folds.

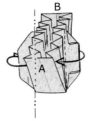

9 At the right, valley the projecting pleat into the line of pleats. At the left, do the same, but with a mountain fold.

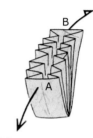

10 Spread AB apart.

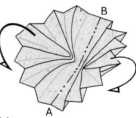

11 Make a straight mountain fold connecting AEB. This will 'snap' the rosette into its final shape. Be forceful!

12 The Rosette complete.

FESTIVE DESIGNS

If you have a party or dinner planned, or if you want to decorate your home for Christmas, there are a number of origami designs that are perfect for these special occasions.

In this section you will find designs for a decorative bauble, an angel that can be designed for Christmas or a christening party,

a party streamer, and a bell that is ideal for a dinner party.

The designs will add a homemade touch to your celebrations, and they are a lot of fun to make, too. So, next time you have a special occasion, be sure to give these a try and impress your family and friends with your origami skills.

BAUBLE

This is stunning decoration for the Christmas tree. This may seem like a complex design, but it is little more than a simple crease pattern repeated many times along the paper. The secret of success is to crease with care and accuracy. Use an oblong of lightweight paper or foil, four times as long as it is wide. For a small bauble, use a piece 30 x 7.5 cm (12 x 3 in), and for a huge one try an oblong measuring 90 x 22.5 cm (36 x 9 in). It is probably easier to start with a medium-sized one. Avoid using papers with a strong decorative pattern – the many facets of the bauble create a strong light and shade pattern of their own, which would clash with colour patterns. To suspend the bauble you will need needle and thread, and some plasticine

1 With the paper right side up, valley fold twice to form three equal sections.

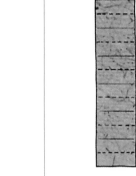

3 Make valley creases midway between the existing creases, creating 12 equal divisions

5 Fold the sheet in half along its length. Unfold.

2 Make valley creases midway between each section, creating six equal divisions.

4 Make valley creases midway between each of the existing creases, creating 24 equal divisions. Keep the folds accurate.

6 Fold the sides into the middle of the sheet, creasing right along its length. Unfold.

7 Look at the crease pattern so far. All the existing creases are valleys, the new ones will be mountains.

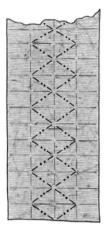

8 Now make careful diagonal mountain folds across the middle, as shown, making sure your folds exactly connect at the intersections of existing creases. It may help to draw the line of the new folds with a pencil before creasing. This is a tricky step. Make sure the creases do not stray towards the outer edges of the sheet, and make them firm.

9 Along the two outer edge sections, re-crease alternate valley creases to make them mountains as shown. This will produce a pleated effect along the edges, with diamonds across the middle. Locate As, Bs, Cs, and Ds.

10 Now squeeze the pleats together on both edges so that the side and end points (C and A) of the diamond rise up, and the middle point (D) of the diamond and pleat (B) cave in.

11 Compress the pleats all along the strip, concertina fashion. Press firmly to reinforce all the creases, and then turn over.

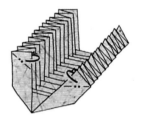

12 Mountain fold the single layer corners inside at both front ends.

13 Valley fold the double layer corners on the inside edges, as shown. Repeat all the way down the row of pleats, neatly folding in each corner in turn.

14 Bring the ends round and together to form the bauble shape.

15 Tuck the left-hand edge under the right, as shown, locking the bauble.

16 The Bauble complete. To hang it, simply use a needle and thread to fix a loop to the top of the bauble. Alternatively, before locking the ends of the bauble together (see Step 15), attach a blob of plasticine to the free ends of a loop of thread and position it inside the body of the bauble, allowing the loop to issue from the top. The locking action will enclose the plasticine and hold the thread firmly in place

ANGEL

This elegant, semi-abstract design is far removed from the literal style of representation seen in some models. It succeeds well in capturing the likeness of a subject with just a few folds – just as difficult as using many. The Angel can be used to decorate the front of a Christmas card, or attached to the top of the Christmas tree with a loop of sticky tape. A rectangle of medium weight paper or foil, proportioned 3:2, or a sheet of A4 or A5 paper are all suitable for this piece.

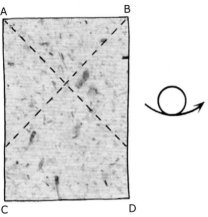

1 Fold A over to the right so that it lies on edge BD. Crease and unfold. Repeat, folding B over to the left to lie on edge AC. Crease, unfold, and turn over.

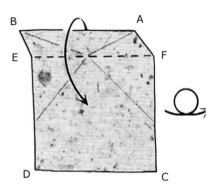

3 Make a horizontal valley fold which passes through the centrepoint of the mountain 'cross'. Turn back over.

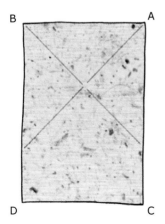

2 The creases now rise towards you.

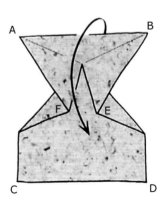

4 Holding the sides of the paper at E and F, let A and B rise up as the sides are brought inwards . . .

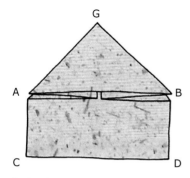

5 ... like this. Flatten the paper.

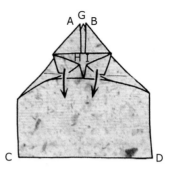

8 Hold G, A and B and swing them back up to where G used to be at the top. Keep a firm hold of them. The paper does not lie flat in the middle.

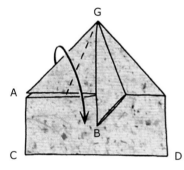

6 Imagine a centre crease from the top point (G) down the middle of the paper. Fold in A and B to lie along that imaginary crease. Keep it neat at G. B has already been folded.

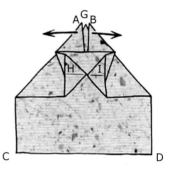

9 Flatten the paper to form triangles H and I. Hold the paper with your left hand at H, and. . .

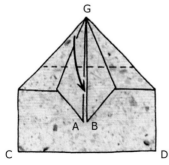

7 Fold G down to AB. Crease firmly.

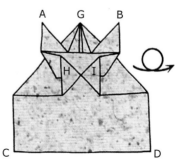

10 ... pull B and A away from G (see the next drawing to check the new position). Flatten and crease. Turn over.

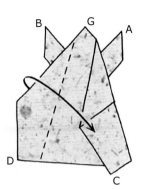

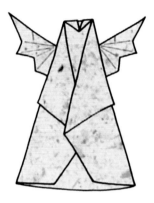

10 ... pull B and A away from G (see the next drawing to check the new position). Flatten and crease. Turn over.

12 The Angel complete.

11 Tuck D and C behind. Fold down G. Carefully pleat the wings.

STREAMER

Here is a model which can be as long as you like! Learn the technique on one strip, fold another, and then join them together by glueing the last pleat of one to the first pleat of another. Repeat as many times as you wish, being careful to fold all sections from identical strips. The result is spectacular. Use a long, narrow strip of lightweight paper or foil, about 8 cm (3 in) wide. As you get more confident, you can experiment by altering the paper width.

1 With the right side of the paper facing you, mountain fold edge AB on a diagonal, so that AB lies under the bottom edge of the strip.

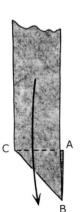

2 Fold the length of the strip down along horizontal crease CA.

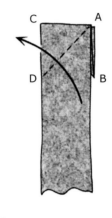

3 Now fold the strip to the left along diagonal crease DA. Be careful to keep all the layers lined up at the edges.

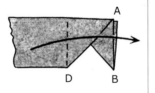

4 Fold the strip to the right, making a vertical crease.

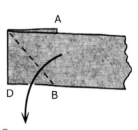

5 Fold the strip down along a diagonal crease. Keep the layers lined up.

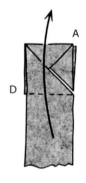

6 Fold the strip back up making a horizontal crease . . .

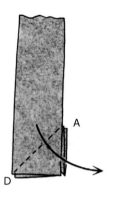

7 ... and then fold to the right along a diagonal crease.

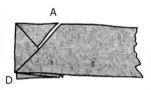

8 Continue the sequence established above until the whole strip is folded up. Be extremely careful to keep all the layers lined up exactly.

9 Unfold the strip to see this crease pattern along the strip.

10 Now mountain fold the other diagonals on each square, all along the strip. Keep it neat, and be careful to make the creases the same way up as the existing diagonals.

11 Fold valley creases through the exact point where the diagonals intersect. Note that both diagonals are mountain creases, and all horizontals are valleys.

12 The creases made in Step 11 form squares along the strip. Mountain fold diagonals on these squares just formed, connecting the top left – to the bottom right-hand corners of each square ...

13 ... and then the top right to the bottom left corners. Keep it neat!

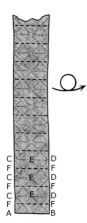

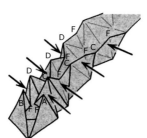

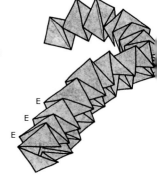

14 Make valley folds midway between the existing valley creases. These new creases each pass through two mountain diagonal 'crosses'. This is the completed crease pattern. Check that when you look at the paper all the diagonal creases are mountains, all the horizontals are valleys, and all the creases join, connect or intersect with accuracy. Identify AB, Cs, Ds, Es and Fs. Turn over.

15 Hold the edges of the strip at the first DC pair along from BA. Push them together gently and E should collapse downwards. Push a few more DC pairs together moving along the strip. F should tuck in and down on top. Continue like this, pushing BA up, to concertina up all the Es and to reinforce the creases. Note that all creases form – nothing is wasted.

16 When concertinaed, the strip will look something like this. Repeat with as many strips of identical width as you wish to fold. Glue them into one enormously long strip. Alternatively, bend one end of the streamer round to meet the other and glue to form a circular decoration. If the creases need to be redefined, push the ends towards each other, squeezing the concertina flat together. The streamer can be stored easily in this position from one Christmas to the next.

BELL

Inflatable origami – blow-ups – are always fun to make, but there are very few such models; the Waterbomb is perhaps the best known. When folding, leave a small hole at the bottom corner to blow into. Do not close it completely by folding too neatly! If the hole is too small, snip it open with scissors. Use a 15-20 cm (6-8 in) square of light – or medium weight paper or foil. To suspend the bell you will need a needle and thread.

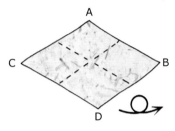

1 Fold horizontal and vertical valley folds across the paper. Turn over, so that the creases rise towards you.

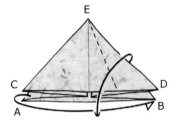

4 Flatten the paper so that two triangles lie either side of the centre.

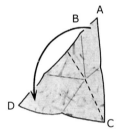

2 Fold A over to D as shown. Unfold. Repeat this move, folding B over to C.

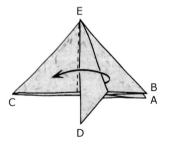

5 Fold D inwards so that edge ED lies along the centre crease. (It may help to mark ABCD in pencil.) Swing A on the left around the back to the right so that it lies behind B.

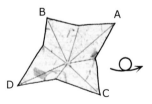

3 The crease pattern should look like this. The paper is three-dimensional. Turn over so that the middle rises up. Push the horizontal and vertical mountain folds towards each other so that the central peak rises up, as shown. Four triangles are formed, meeting at E.

6 Swing D over to the left.

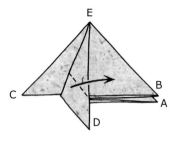

7 Fold up D as shown so that it lies along edge CB.

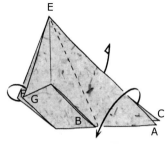

10 As in Step 5, fold A inwards so that edge EA lies along the centre crease, covering B. Swing F on the left around the back to lie hidden behind C on the right. Swing A over to the left to lie on top of G. Fold up A like D in Step 7.

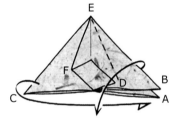

8 The paper now looks like this. The folds in Steps 5-7 are now repeated with B, then A and then C. As in Step 5, fold B inwards so that edge EB lies along the centre crease, covering D. Swing C on the left around the back to lie behind A on the right.

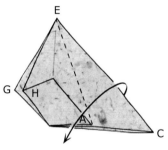

11 As in Step 5, fold C inwards so that edge EC lies along the centre crease, covering A.

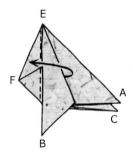

9 Swing B over to the left to lie on top of F. Fold up B like D in Step 7.

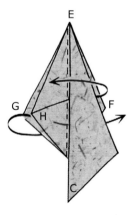

12 Swing G on the left around the back and to the right to lie behind F. Swing C over to the left, to lie on top of H.

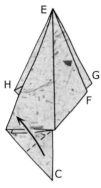

13 Fold up corner C, as shown. Crease flat.

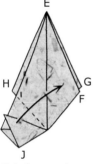

14 Fold the flap up as shown ...

15 ... and slide J under the edge that runs down the centre of the paper, pushing it deep into the pocket.

16 The paper is now symmetrical. Carefully form valley creases between and K and H and K on the left and mountain creases between F and K and G and K on the right. Do not crease beyond the centre.

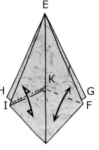

17 Now make mountain creases on the left and valleys on the right, placing these creases on top of the previous ones. This will form creases that can bend backwards and forwards. Bend them to and fro several times so that they are very flexible.

18 At the bottom end, there should be a small hole. Blow into it and the bell should inflate! Inflating it is easier if the four flaps are spread apart and if the hole is clearly visible. The flexible creases just made will form a definite rim to the bell.

19 The Bell complete. To suspend, attach a loop to the top of the bell with needle and thread.

STAR

A good way to form geometric shapes is to fold a number of simple shapes which can interlock. This is commonly known as 'modular origami'. The Star is a simple example of this kind of folding, and to experiment try folding six, eight or more modules to make stars with more than four points. You will need four sheets of lightweight paper or foil about 10 cm (4 in) square in two colours or textures which work well together. Choosing complementary papers with care always adds to the finished piece. To suspend the star you will need a needle and thread.

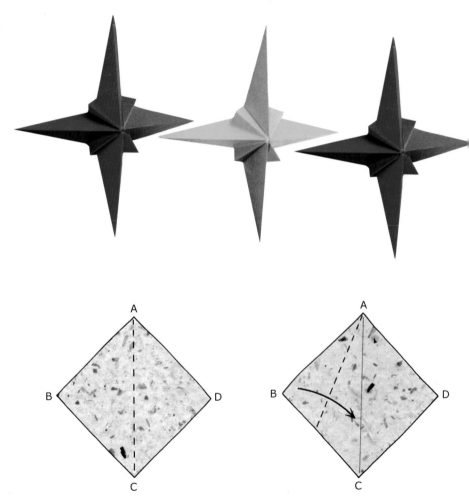

1 Fold B over to D. Crease and unfold.

2 Fold in edge AB to lie along crease AC.

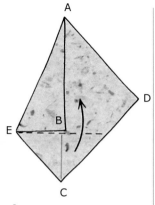

3 Fold up C along a crease which follows edge EB, covering B.

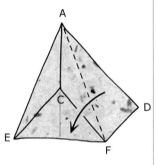

4 Fold in edge AD to the centre so that it half covers C.

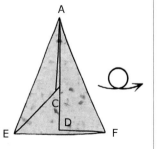

5 The paper looks like this. Turn over.

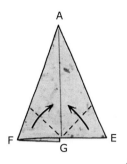

6 Fold in F and E to lie along crease AG.

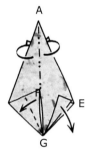

7 Fold F and E back out to the sloping edges just formed which meet at G. E is shown already folded. Keep the folds neat at G.

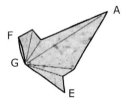

8 Unfold the last two steps so it looks like this. This is one point of the star. Make three more sections just the same as the first, but make two of them in another (maybe patterned) paper.

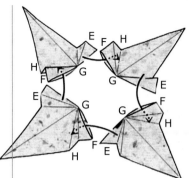

9 Tuck corner E of one section in between the layers of another at F and continue to push it further in until E touches H and the two Gs touch. The mountain and valley creases should line up where they overlap. In the same way, tuck in the third and fourth sections, alternating the types of paper, and finally locking the first section into the fourth. Strengthen and sharpen all the creases.

10 The Star complete. To suspend, attach a loop to one point of the star with needle and thread.

SIX-POINTED STAR

One of the simplest and most attractive of all folded decorations, the six-pointed star uses the most basic folding techniques. Steps 1-4 show how to make an equilateral triangle (one with all its sides of equal length) from a square. If you know another method of doing this by all means use it, although the one shown here is accurate and pleasing. Make several stars, in an array of bright colours, and hang from the Christmas tree for extra sparkle. Use a square of paper of any weight or size. The best paper to use for this decoration is paper-backed metallic foil, which reflects the light and will make the star stand out against the dark foliage of a natural Christmas tree. Scissors, needle and thread.

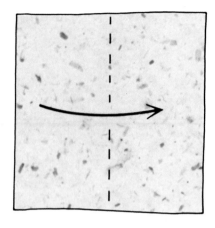

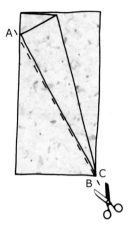

1 Fold in half, left to right.

3 Cut along edge BA, Open out the bottom left-hand triangle and discard the remainder of the paper. Add creases which run into corners B and C to locate the centre of the triangle.

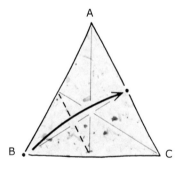

4 Fold B across to the opposite edge.

2 Turn in the top layer corner to exactly touch the crease made in Step 1, at such a point that the new crease will run exactly down to the bottom corner. Take your time lining it up – this is the most important crease in the whole design. Badly placed, it will spoil the shape of the star.

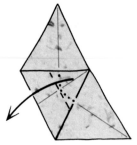

5 Fold B back along a crease which passes over the centre of the triangle.

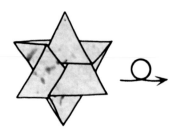

8 Like this. Turn over.

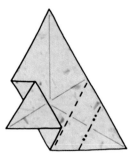

6 Repeat Steps 4 and 5 with C.

9 The Six-Pointed Star complete. To suspend, attach a loop to the star with needle and thread. The star looks most effective when hung in groups.

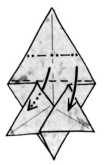

7 Repeat Steps 4 and 5 with A. Tuck the left-hand part of the pleat under B to lock A B and C together in a symmetrical pattern.

INDEX

A

Architectural Module, 94
  Bar Module: End Lock, 95
  Bar Module: End and Side Locks, 97
  Bar Module: Side Lock, 96
  Corner Junction, 99
  Four Way Junction, 98

B

Barking Dog, 100-1
Basic Techniques
  Outside Reverse Fold, 14
  Reverse Fold, 12-3
  Squash Fold, 15

E

Eastern Designs, 40
  Cat, 54-5
  Cube, 52-3
  Eternally Opening Origami, 50-1
  Fox, 64-5
  Incense Burner, 56-9
  Mount Fuji and the Sea, 46-7
  Stretch wall, 66-9
  Tulip and Stem, 60-3
  Yacht, 48-9
  Yoshizawa's Butterflies, 41-5

F

Festive Designs, 106
  Angel, 10-13
  Bauble, 107-9
  Bell, 118-21
  Six-pointed Star, 124-25
  Star, 122-23
  Streamer, 114-17

First Principles
  How to make a crease, 11
  How to make a square, 10

I

Introduction, 6
  Paper, 7
  Symbols, 8-9

R

Rosette, 104-5
Rowing Boat, 102-3

T

Traditional Designs, 16
  Banger, 17
  Bird, 20-1
  Crane, 30-1
  Crown, 18-9
  Cup, 22-3
  Dish, 26-7
  Flapping bird, 28-9
  Glider, 32-3
  Junk, 36-9
  Sampan, 34-5
  Waterlilly, 24-5

W

Western Designs, 70
  Arrow, 71
  Daffodil, 88-93
  Face, 76-9
  Pop-up double cube, 82-5
  Rooster, 80-1
  Snap Hexahedron, 72-3
  Star, 86-7
  Un-unfoldable Box, 74-5

ACKNOWLEDGEMENTS

Thank you to those origami creators who gave me permission to publish their wonderful designs. In particular, I must thank the Japanese Living Treasure of origami, Akira Yoshizawa, for his permission to publish his Butterfly and for his generous support of the book. Florence Temko's Rooster was first published in her book Pandas and Jumping Frogs, China Books, USA.

ORIGAMI SOCIETIES

Here are addresses for two societies which cater well for the beginner. If you would like to know more about origami, both publish informative magazines and organise regional and national meetings. Membership to both is worldwide.
British Origami Society
253 Park Lane
Poynton
Stockport SK12 1RH
England

The Friends of the Origami Center of America
15 West 77th Street
New York
NY 10024
USA